# Gods and Goddesses of Ancient Egypt

*An Enthralling Overview of the Most Important Deities in Egyptian Mythology*

© Copyright 2025 - All rights reserved.

The content contained within this book may not be reproduced, duplicated, or transmitted without direct written permission from the author or the publisher.

Under no circumstances will any blame or legal responsibility be held against the publisher, or author, for any damages, reparation, or monetary loss due to the information contained within this book, either directly or indirectly.

**Legal Notice:**

This book is copyright protected. It is only for personal use. You cannot amend, distribute, sell, use, quote, or paraphrase any part, or the content within this book, without the consent of the author or publisher.

**Disclaimer Notice:**

Please note the information contained within this document is for educational and entertainment purposes only. All effort has been executed to present accurate, up-to-date, reliable, and complete information. No warranties of any kind are declared or implied. Readers acknowledge that the author is not engaging in the rendering of legal, financial, medical, or professional advice. The content within this book has been derived from various sources. Please consult a licensed professional before attempting any techniques outlined in this book.

By reading this document, the reader agrees that under no circumstances is the author responsible for any losses, direct or indirect, that are incurred as a result of the use of the information contained within this document, including, but not limited to, errors, omissions, or inaccuracies.

# Free limited time bonus

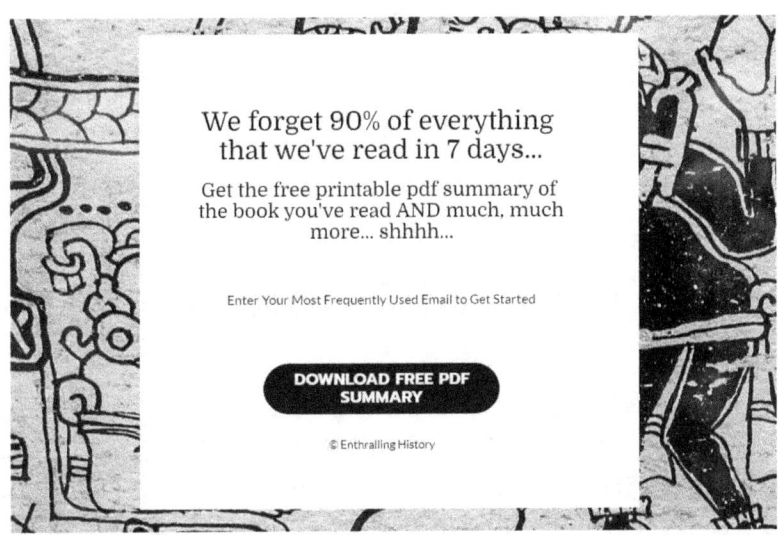

Stop for a moment. We have a free bonus set up for you. The problem is this: we forget 90% of everything that we read after 7 days. Crazy fact, right? Here's the solution: we've created a printable, 1-page pdf summary for this book that you're reading now. All you have to do to get your free pdf summary is to go to the following website: **https://livetolearn.lpages.co/enthrallinghistory/**

Or, Scan the QR code!

Once you do, it will be intuitive. Enjoy, and thank you!

# Table of Contents

INTRODUCTION ..................................................................................... 1
CHAPTER 1: THE ORIGINS OF EGYPTIAN MYTHOLOGY ............... 3
CHAPTER 2: THE SUN AND THE SKY: RA AND NUT ....................... 9
CHAPTER 3: CHAOS AND ORDER: SET AND OSIRIS ..................... 19
CHAPTER 4: LOVE AND MAGIC: ISIS ............................................... 29
CHAPTER 5: THE GOD OF MUMMIFICATION: ANUBIS ................ 38
CHAPTER 6: THE GUARDIANS OF ORDER: THOTH AND MA'AT ... 48
CHAPTER 7: HORUS THE FALCON KING ........................................ 58
CHAPTER 8: SERPENT MAGIC AND TRANSFORMATION: WADJET AND SOBEK ......................................................................... 66
CHAPTER 9: LESSER-KNOWN DEITIES: A CASE STUDY .............. 76
CHAPTER 10: THE IMPACT OF EGYPTIAN MYTHOLOGY ON MODERN CULTURE ........................................................................... 87
CONCLUSION ..................................................................................... 92
HERE'S ANOTHER BOOK BY ENTHRALLING HISTORY THAT YOU MIGHT LIKE .............................................................................. 94
FREE LIMITED TIME BONUS ........................................................... 95
BIBLIOGRAPHY .................................................................................. 96
IMAGE SOURCES ............................................................................... 98

# Introduction

From the towering pyramids touching the sky to the mysterious Sphinx guarding the vast Giza Plateau, the symbols of ancient Egypt have long captivated the imagination of the world. Yet, beyond these popular monuments lies a realm even more fascinating: the pantheon of Egyptian gods and goddesses. Many may be familiar with names like Osiris, Isis, Anubis, and Ra, perhaps from a passing reference in a movie, a depiction in a comic strip, or as dramatic characters in a fantasy novel. However, the true essence of these deities is far more complex and compelling than these modern interpretations often suggest.

Just as Norse and Greek mythologies are preserved in poems or hymns, the heart of Egyptian mythology also beats in texts. The Book of the Dead, the Pyramid Texts, and the Coffin Texts are a few examples of the ancient manuscripts that offer us a window into the Egyptian understanding of the cosmos, the afterlife, and the divine.

The ancient Egyptians did not see their gods and goddesses as mere symbols or abstract concepts; they were integral to every part of their lives, from the flooding of the Nile to the changing of seasons and from birth to death. Because of this, they took extreme care to please the divine, hoping their offerings and dedications could steer them away from the wrath of the gods. There was a time when they once abandoned a shrine of a mighty god. Perhaps as a punishment, the Egyptians had to go through seven years of drought and famine. Surprisingly, the event of the drought was historically correct and recorded in the Famine Stela excavated near Aswan.

Moreover, the relationship between these gods and goddesses reflects the intricacies of human relationships. The legend of Osiris's resurrection, for instance, unfolds not only a tale of betrayal and power struggle but also provides valuable lessons surrounding the themes of love, order, and the cycle of life. Similarly, the rivalry between Horus and Set mirrors the human struggles between order and chaos and good and evil.

To put it simply, understanding Egyptian mythology offers more than just a glimpse into ancient beliefs; it also provides a window into the worldview of one of the most fascinating civilizations in human history. It unveils how the ancient Egyptians interpreted the world around them, how they made sense of natural phenomena, and how they sought to understand their place in the vast universe.

This book aims to unravel the intricate web of stories, legends, and beliefs that form the Egyptian pantheon. It delves into the origins of the world according to Egyptian lore, the roles of various gods and goddesses of the pantheon—from the most famous ones to less-prominent and nearly forgotten deities—and their journeys and adventures in a time long past. Through this book, readers will discover the layers of each deity's nature, including how gods like Sobek are embodiments of protection and fertility and why a god was often seen as unpredictable. Of course, there will be a few details and legends you may already know, but there will hopefully be something waiting inside this book that might surprise you.

# Chapter 1: The Origins of Egyptian Mythology

The story of how the world came to be cannot be explained in just a single page. While some believe it all began with an empty canvas or perhaps a dark expanse of nothingness, others chose not to describe the beginning at all, believing that the origin was too sacred and complex or too unknowable to be spoken aloud. The ancient Egyptians, however, thought otherwise. They had three narratives to explain the genesis of everything.

Those who hailed from the once glimmering city of the sun, Heliopolis, believed that everything started with the god Atum, who carved out the world from a primordial hill. Those in Memphis, on the other hand, held the god of craftsmen, Ptah, in high regard, while Egyptians in Hermopolis believed that the creation of the world had something to do with the Ogdoad, eight deities who existed in perfect balance with each other.

### The Heliopolitan Creation Myth

Of course, just like other creation stories from various civilizations across the globe, the ancient Egyptians also believed that their story began with a vast expanse of nothingness where silence reigned supreme. According to this version, the first stirrings of creation began in the ancient city of Heliopolis. Once a major city of the ancient kingdom, it had been occupied as early as the time of prehistoric Egypt. However, the name Heliopolis was Greek (it means the "city of the sun"). To the ancient Egyptians, the city was known as Lunu, which translates to the "pillar city." The city was of great importance. According to their beliefs, Heliopolis was the location where the sun's rays first kissed the earth and where legends of their gods and goddesses first unfolded.

Long before the land was dotted with obelisks and grand temples with towering statues, there existed only Nun, the primordial waters of chaos. These waters, dark and unfathomable, held within them the potential of all that was to be. In this boundless sea of possibility, an event would take place that would change the course of existence forever: the emergence of the very first piece of land, a sacred mound rising from the depths of Nun.

Atum, who later merged with the sun god Ra to become Atum-Ra, the first and most ancient of the Egyptian gods, came into being upon this mound. However, Atum, in his solitude, yearned for more than just existence. He yearned for life, for creation, and for the company of others.

And so, in a feat of divine power, Atum began the act of creation. From his own essence, he brought forth the first pair of deities: Shu, the god of air, and Tefnut, the goddess of moisture. Shu, with his breath of life, then filled the space between the heavens and the earth, while Tefnut brought the principle of order, weaving it delicately into the canvas of creation.

At one point, Shu and Tefnut were said to have disappeared when they went to explore the primeval waters, leaving Atum alone yet again. Perhaps desperate to cure his sadness and find his children, Atum sent forth the Eye of Ra (a divine entity often depicted as either the sun disk or the right Wedjat eye), which scholars often interpret to be synonymous with the goddess Hathor in certain myths.

The Eye of Ra was powerful and all-seeing. It journeyed through the chaos of Nun, illuminating the shadows and peering into the hidden crevices of the primordial sea. Back in the world, Atum waited, his heart heavy with worry and longing.

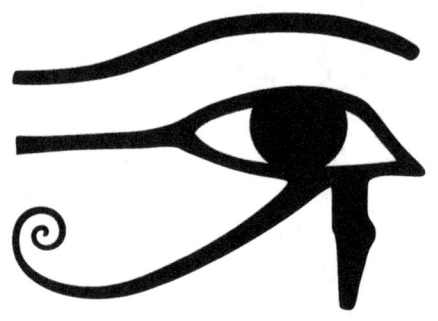

**Symbol of the Eye of Ra.**[1]

The Eye of Ra was successful in its quest. It returned with Shu and Tefnut to the sacred mound of creation. Atum's heart swelled with joy and relief. Overcome with happiness at the return of his children, tears streamed from his eyes, falling upon the fertile earth of the mound. From these tears of joy, something miraculous occurred. Where each tear touched the earth, the dirt transformed, taking shape and life. These droplets also became the first humans.

Shu and Tefnut then gave birth to more divine beings. Geb was the god of the earth, while Nut was the goddess of the sky. Now, in ancient Egyptian beliefs, unions between siblings were common. For gods and mortal royals, it was thought to be a way to preserve their sacred lineage. And so, despite being siblings, Geb and Nut were joined as a divine couple. It was through them that the fundamental structure of the world was finally established. Geb (the earth) and Nut (the heavens above) were forever bound but eternally separated by their father, Shu.

However, Geb and Nut were not barren. Their union led to the birth of four more children, each with destinies that would further shape the world. Osiris was the firstborn son who soon became crowned the first king of Egypt. His position was not permanent, as he would embark on a journey to transform into the ruler of the underworld. Their second child was Isis, who was also the wife of Osiris. She was hailed as the goddess of magic and healing, and her wisdom was said to be as deep as the Nile itself. The third was Set, the god of chaos and storms. Although often thought to have brought destruction, Set was also crucial in bringing change, balance, and renewal. Last but not least was the goddess Nephthys. The wife of Set, Nephthys was associated with mourning and the protective care of the dead.

Along with Atum, Shu, Tefnut, Geb, and Nut, these nine gods formed the Great Ennead. They completed the creation of the world in their own ways. While Osiris introduced knowledge of agriculture, teaching mankind the ways of planting and harvesting to ensure their survival, Isis shared her sacred knowledge of magic. The goddess taught humans the art of medicine, as well as the ways of domestication. Set, on the other hand, had a complex role in shaping the world. He brought storms and upheavals. These were not always a form of destruction; they also served as a form of renewal and necessary disruption. Challenging the order of things was the only way to ensure that balance could be restored and maintained. Meanwhile, his wife, Nephthys, played a quieter role. She provided solace to the souls in the afterlife, ensuring their safe passage to the beyond.

## The Memphite Creation Myth

While Atum was the main figure of the Heliopolis creation myth, this next tale of creation revolved around Ptah, the patron god of craftsmen and architects. In contrast to the story of Atum and the Heliopolis, this particular creation myth focused more on the power of the mind and speech.

Ptah was the patron god of Memphis. According to Memphite theology, the god created the world simply using his heart and tongue. Of course, this is not to be taken literally; he did not sacrifice his body parts to shape the world, like how the Norse god Odin created the world using the body of the primordial frost giant, Ymir. The ancient Egyptians held strong to the belief that the heart was the very seat of thought and the source of all intentions and ideas. The tongue then gave these thoughts form and reality through speech. Therefore, together, they became the tools of creation. To put it simply, the mighty Ptah thought about creating the world and spoke it into existence. Since this creation myth also coexisted with that of Heliopolis, some even claimed that it was Ptah who uttered the words that led to the creation of Atum.

Every god, river, star, and living being started as a thought in Ptah's heart. When he spoke, these thoughts emerged from the void of nothingness and began taking form and substance. Now that Ptah was no longer alone, as he was accompanied by the gods who had been born from his own words, the responsibilities to shape the world were split between them. Some became rulers, while others were caretakers of the various elements and aspects of the world.

Interestingly, in comparison to the Heliopolitan creation story, Ptah's version did not gain the same widespread acceptance among the majority of the ancient Egyptians. This was largely due to the fact that the Heliopolitan myth was bolstered by the political and religious influence of Heliopolis itself. The city was a religious and cultural center of the ancient Egyptians for a long time.

## Hermopolitan Creation Myth

The last creation myth presents a rather unique perspective on the origin of the cosmos. The Hermopolitan narrative actually has a few different versions, each captivating in its own right.

The first version gave the spotlight to the Ogdoad, a group of eight deities, four males and their four female counterparts. These gods represented the fundamentals of chaos: water, darkness, infinity, and mystery. They were Nun and Naunet (representing the primeval waters), Amun and Amaunet (the water's hidden and mysterious nature), Huh and Hauhet (the water's infinity), and Kek and Kauket (darkness of the water). The Ogdoad as a whole was believed to have dwelled in the depths of Nun, the chaotic waters that existed before creation.

A depiction of the Ogdoad at the Hathor Temple in Dendera. The male deities were often depicted with frog heads, while their female counterparts had serpent heads.'

It was within this realm of chaos and nothingness that a mystical event occurred. From the interactions of these eight divine beings, a great mound emerged. Almost immediately, it broke the endless surface of the stagnant waters. This was the start of creation. It was also believed that these eight gods were the earliest to have ruled the earth. However, these primordial deities were not immortal. When their time had passed, the Ogdoad moved to the underworld, or the Du'at, where they resided for eternity.

Still, their task was far from over. From this new residence, the Ogdoad kept their eyes wide open, ensuring that the sun rose every day. As long as they were in power, the Ogdoad would make sure that the Nile continued to flow, ensuring the Egyptians could see the inundation visit their crops every year.

Meanwhile, there was also another version of the Hermopolitan creation story that spoke of how the world came from a cosmic egg. The egg itself was said to have been created either by the Ogdoad or laid by a long-forgotten celestial goose named the Gengen-Wer. From this divine egg came Ra, the mighty sun god, who then worked to create the world and everything else in it.

As the narratives evolved, the Ogdoad, which were initially central to the Hermopolitan myth, gradually faded from the official Egyptian pantheon, though their names remained in oral and written legends. Of course, their names were not entirely forgotten. Instead, they were overshadowed by the growing influence of other powerful deities, especially Ra. The falcon-headed sun god would be placed at the top of the pantheon, becoming chief of all Egyptian gods.

Narratives and legends in Egypt never stopped evolving, especially when the kingdom entered a new era. The New Kingdom period, for instance, saw the emergence of yet another creator deity. Known as Amun-Ra (the amalgamation of the god Amun and Ra), the deity was thought to be a self-created being and the ultimate originator of all that exists. He was often depicted as an invisible force or a hidden god whose power and presence permeated the entire universe itself. This narrative was accepted widely, especially at Karnak, the religious center of the kingdom at the time.

Another creation narrative that surfaced during this period involved the god named Khnum. Depicted with the head of a ram, the god was mainly worshiped on the island of Elephantine. According to this myth, Khnum used his divine potter's wheel to create the very first humans. In comparison to the other creation myths, this particular story emphasizes not how the earth and its elements came to be but rather the individuality of each human life and the careful attention of the divine in the creation process.

# Chapter 2: The Sun and the Sky: Ra and Nut

The ancient Egyptians were exceptional farmers. Perhaps it was true that they were bestowed the sacred knowledge of agriculture by Osiris himself since they knew exactly how to make use of the resources and fertile lands that the gods had given them. The fertile banks of the Nile, in particular, were the greatest witness to the Egyptians' agricultural prowess. Rejuvenated by the river's annual flooding, these fields were often filled with an abundance of crops, especially wheat and barley—these two were the staples of their diet. Flax, which painted the Egyptian landscape in hues of subtle green, was also a popular crop. With its slender stems, the fiber of this crop was spun into fine linen. The ancient Egyptians also grew tall papyrus plants, which were then turned into papers and scrolls. This allowed them to record the civilization's greatest tales, feats, and history.

This abundance in agriculture did more than just feed the people. In fact, agriculture was the heart of the Egyptian economy. The kingdom thrived and was so wealthy in natural resources to the point that it eventually caught the attention of many other colossal powers at the time. The mighty Romans and the fierce Assyrians, for instance, were among the biggest rivals of the kingdom; they were aware that to control the fertile lands meant absolute wealth and power.

It is also clear that the ancient Egyptians were religious. Despite their busy schedules of toiling the land or sculpting statues of their pharaohs, they never failed to spare some time to look up at the sky and say their gratitude to the mighty sun. To them, the sun was not merely a burning star in the heavens. They viewed the sun with great reverence. After all, it was the sun that showed them when to plant and when to harvest. It was also the sun that had kept them alive and ensured their land was so fertile.

The ancient Egyptians were also very superstitious. Failing to respect and show their gratitude to certain elements of the divine would undoubtedly result in misfortune. The sun was no exception; disrespecting it could easily result in their lives being turned upside down. Drought could replace the inundation that nourished their crops, leaving them with nothing but starvation and catastrophe.

And so, they placed the god Ra on the highest throne of the Egyptian pantheon. He was the embodiment of the great sun itself, whose existence brought light, warmth, and growth. The Egyptians respected the divine being, especially since he was a constant companion in their journey through the seasons.

Ra was often depicted in many forms, each symbolizing his immense power. However, more often than not, Ra appeared on reliefs, texts, and sculptures as a man with the head of a falcon. On his head, he typically wore a sun disk encircled by a cobra, which signified his royal status and divine nature. This image of Ra could be seen etched on the walls of many temples and tombs in Egypt. The most significant site dedicated to the god was the Sun Temple at Heliopolis. Also known as one of the oldest cities in Egypt, Heliopolis was the center of Ra's veneration. Although the state of both the temple and the city is today only a shadow of its former glory, back then, it was undoubtedly a sight to behold. The temple complex once featured towering obelisks that pierced the sky,

A depiction of Ra, the chief god of the Egyptian pantheon.[8]

along with sets of colossal statues that stood as an homage to the mighty Ra. What is left for us today, unfortunately, is only ruins and dust.

Other than being carved onto walls of tombs and temples, Ra's image could also be found on an array of intricate artifacts like amulets, statuettes, and colorful paintings on the surface of a sarcophagus. These artifacts did not serve only as decoration. Most of them were used as talismans of protection; the ancient Egyptians would use them to invoke Ra's power against evil or chaos.

Jewelry featuring Ra adorned with the sun disk and holding the ankh.'

Being one of the superior gods in the Egyptian pantheon, it is not surprising that Ra features in multiple myths. The most popular one tells the story of an aging Ra. After he grew weary of ruling the earth for many centuries, Ra chose to ascend to the heavens. He did not hang his weapons once he got there; instead, Ra continued to reign from above.

Ra would embark on a grand voyage across the sky every day, from dawn until dusk. According to ancient texts, his solar vessel was known as the Mandjet, the "Boat of Millions of Years." It was described to be magnificent; it was made of gold and adorned with precious stone. His trip during the day was nearly free from obstacles. However, when twilight descended, the god's journey took a darker turn. This was also the time when Ra would transform into his alternative appearance: a man with the head of a ram. Aboard a different vessel known as the Mesektet Barque, Ra would plunge beyond the horizon and into the waters, eventually arriving in the bleak underworld.

Ra, in his ram-headed form, traveling through the underworld on the Mesektet Barque.⁵

The journey was far from being a simple walk in the park. In this realm, the sun god had to pass through twelve gates of the underworld, each leading to a different region. While some accounts suggest that the god took at least an hour to reach each gate, others claimed he took longer. During this part of the journey, Ra was said to have paid his respects to Osiris, the god of the underworld himself.

Ra was the chief god of the Egyptian pantheon, but this status alone did not guarantee his fate—and, by extension, the world's fate. The god had to be extra vigilant the entire time he was in the underworld, especially when he was a short distance away from reaching the exit. The nearer he got to the end of the underworld, the closer he was to meeting his greatest enemy of all time: Apophis.

Also known as Apep, this divine entity was a colossal serpent (sometimes depicted as a massive cobra) that represented darkness, chaos, and disorder. Its only task was to battle Ra as he passed through the underworld. The giant serpent wanted to devour the sun and plunge the world into eternal darkness where nothing could survive. Every night, Ra would fight fiercely against him. The sun god would win each night, and Apophis would slither back into hiding, preparing himself for yet another encounter with Ra the next day.

However, there were times when the battle took place slightly differently. Apophis would sometimes gain the upper hand and succeed in swallowing Ra. Without the sun god, the earth was thrown into darkness and uncertainty. Today, this event is recognized as a solar eclipse.

Of course, Ra could not be defeated permanently. Legend has it that whenever this happened, Ra had the help of other deities, particularly Set. It was said that despite Apophis's colossal size, he was incapable of holding Ra in his stomach for too long. The serpent would eventually regurgitate the sun god, allowing Ra to break free and emerge victorious each time. With the battle won, Ra would transform back into his falcon-headed form and board the Mandjet. He would then continue his journey across the sky, bringing forth light and warmth to the people once again. The first light of dawn was seen by the Egyptians as a sign that order had been restored and the cycle of day and night would continue.

Apophis or Apep based on a depiction in the tomb of pharaoh Ramesses I.⁶

As time passed, the Egyptians began to merge Ra with other deities, creating amalgamations that reflected the evolving religious and political landscape. By the time of the New Kingdom, the Egyptians saw the rising prominence of a god named Amun. Originally a local god of Thebes, Amun gained more and more worshipers over time, and his influence eventually rivaled that of Ra. By the 16th century BCE, the two gods had merged, becoming Amun-Ra, which became a symbol of unified divine power.

Amun-Ra seated on his throne.[7]

Some might mistakenly think that Amun-Ra was a different name for Ra. He was more than that, though, at least in the eyes of the ancient Egyptians. Amun-Ra was a complex divine being that represented both the invisible forces of creation (Amun) and the visible source of life (Ra). Even his depictions in temples and inscriptions appeared different compared to Ra. Most of the time, he was often pictured as a man wearing a crown with two tall plumes. Amun-Ra could also bear features of both deities at the same time. Since he was also associated with fertility, he could appear as a ram (rams were regarded as symbols of fertility, rebirth, and resurrection back then) with either curved horns or a sun disk on his head like Ra.

Ra's influence also extended to the pharaohs. To elevate their status, these Egyptian rulers would typically align themselves closely with the sun god. It was common for the pharaohs to see themselves as earthly embodiments of Ra. Pharaohs would often incorporate Ra's name into their own to further solidify their sacred association with the mighty god. Ramesses II (also known as Ramesses the Great) is a great example of this since his name means "Born of Ra."

Being one of the most celebrated pharaohs of ancient Egypt, it is not surprising that Ramesses II's name is familiar to many. Not only did he expand the borders of Egypt and lead his people into a period of stability, but the great pharaoh also left a lasting legacy in the realm of Egyptian architecture. The temple of Abu Simbel is one of the greatest examples of Egyptian architecture. Carved out of a mountainside, the temple features colossal statues of the pharaoh himself seated alongside Amun-Ra and Ptah.

The most remarkable feature of Abu Simbel, however, is its alignment with the sun. Twice a year, on February $22^{nd}$ and October $22^{nd}$, the sun's rays penetrate the inner sanctum of the temple, illuminating the statues of Ramesses and Amun-Ra while leaving the statue of Ptah, the god of darkness, in shadow. This spectacular phenomenon is not just an architectural marvel. Many saw it as a representation of Ra's journey through the sky and the underworld.

### Nut, the Egyptian Sky Goddess

Nut was often portrayed as a woman stretched over the earth god Geb, enveloping him and all his creatures in a protective embrace. Her body, a vast canopy adorned with stars, represented the night sky. This image of Nut arching over the earth was not just a representation of the sky; it was also a symbol of her all-encompassing protection and the eternal cycle of day and night. In some depictions, Nut took the form of a cow or a sow, signifying her role as the mother of the gods. This maternal aspect was a vital part of her identity, highlighting her nurturing nature and her role in giving birth to and protecting the celestial bodies.

The ladder, or Maqet, is another sacred symbol associated with Nut. It represented the stairway to heaven, which was believed to help the deceased reach the goddess's domain. It was believed to be used by Osiris to ascend into her heavenly domain. This symbol was often placed in tombs as a means of protection for the deceased, ensuring their safe passage into the afterlife under Nut's watchful gaze. Egyptian artists also portrayed Nut as a woman holding a pot of water, which represented her role as the giver of rain, essential for the fertility and sustenance of the earth.

Nut, arching over Geb, supported by the god of air, Shu.⁸

Pepi I Meryre, the third pharaoh of the Sixth Dynasty of Egypt, held Nut in such high regard. This deep reverence could be seen on the walls of his tomb chamber, which were heavily adorned with a collection of Pyramid Texts dedicated to the goddess. These texts included a hymn to Nut, which was more than just a set of verses. It was also a sacred invocation, a plea for protection, and a celebration of Nut's divine nature. The walls transformed the tomb into a sanctum of celestial magic, aligning the resting place of the pharaoh with the heavenly realm of Nut.

The integration of the hymn in Pepi I's tomb highlights the enduring influence of Nut in Egyptian religious practices, particularly concerning the afterlife. The pharaoh's association with Nut in his eternal resting place was believed to ensure his safe passage through the night sky and secure his rebirth in the afterlife.

Despite her important role in mythology and art, the worship of Nut was not as common as that of other Egyptian deities. Her presence was more ethereal, tied to the cosmos and the natural world rather than the more tangible aspects of daily life.

Nut's role in the cosmos was tied to her relationship with Ra, the sun god. As the sky goddess, she played a critical role in the cycle of the sun and, by extension, the cycle of life and death.

One of the most captivating myths involving Nut is her role in the sun's rebirth. Each evening, as Ra completed his journey across the sky, he would descend into Nut's embrace. She would then swallow him, marking the end of the day and the beginning of the night. In the depths of Nut's celestial body, Ra would travel through the night, undergoing a process of renewal and rebirth. Come dawn, Nut would give birth to Ra once again. He would be reborn and revitalized and begin his new journey across the sky.

**Nut swallowing the sun, allowing it to travel through her body at night and be reborn at dawn.**[9]

Nut's role in this process was very important. She was the guardian of the sun during the vulnerable hours of the night. She was the nurturer who ensured its rejuvenation and the birth-giver who brought forth the sun with the new day. However, Ra was not always on the same page as Nut. The two gods once had a major disagreement.

Nut was married to Geb, the god of earth, who was also her brother. They were said to be deeply in love. However, Ra did not bless their union. Some claim that the sun god was deeply enamored with Nut, while others suggested that Ra was fearful of a prophecy that a child of

Nut would one day surpass him. Whatever the reason was, the sun god was said to have placed a curse upon Nut. He decreed that the sky goddess could not give birth to her children any day of the year. This curse was a devastating blow to Nut.

In her distress, Nut turned to Thoth, the god of wisdom and knowledge, for assistance. Thoth, known for his cleverness, devised a plan to outwit Ra's curse. He challenged Khonsu, the moon god, to a game of senet, a popular board game in ancient Egypt. Thoth was a master of the game and won several rounds, each time claiming a small portion of Khonsu's lunar light as his prize.

With the light he won, Thoth created five extra days, known as the "epagomenal days," which were not part of the regular Egyptian calendar year. This ingenious solution effectively circumvented Ra's curse since these days existed outside the bounds of the established year.

During these five magical days, Nut was able to give birth to her five children: Osiris, Horus the Elder (not to be confused with the falcon god of the same name), Set, Isis, and Nephthys. Each was born on a separate day. Osiris, born on the first of these days, grew up to become an important figure in Egyptian mythology. He is often associated with resurrection and the afterlife. Horus the Elder, Set, Isis, and Nephthys each played their own unique role in the pantheon.

News of the birth of these gods eventually reached Ra. Upon learning about the tricks that Nut and Thoth had pulled to evade his curse, the sun god flew into a rage. Fueled by anger and a sense of betrayal, Ra made a momentous decision that would forever alter the fabric of the cosmos and the fate of the two lovers, Nut and Geb.

Ra summoned Shu, the god of the air and wind, and gave him a daunting task. He ordered Shu to stand forever between Nut and Geb, ensuring that the sky and the earth would be separated. This decree forever changed the natural order and the lives of Nut and Geb.

Shu, bound by his duty to Ra, obeyed the command. He positioned himself beneath Nut, lifting her high above. Nut arched gracefully across the heavens and became the sky itself. Below her, Geb lay as the earth, sprawling and verdant, forever gazing up at his beloved yet never able to join her.

This separation of Nut and Geb explained the fundamental structure of the world. It was a powerful and poetic image as well: the sky and the earth, two eternal lovers, close yet forever apart.

# Chapter 3: Chaos and Order: Set and Osiris

According to mythology, Osiris was Egypt's very first king. He was the first to unite Egypt and rule humankind. Osiris was so kind and fair that the ancient Egyptians held him in high regard. He was praised for his wisdom, justice, and nurturing spirit. Under his benevolent reign, the people knew no chaos. War was not common, and it seemed as if peace would be everlasting. The Nile's waters never failed to flood the fields, allowing the granaries of Egypt to be overflowed with bountiful harvests. Osiris was also believed to have been the one to have taught humans the art of agriculture and civilization. These precious contributions made him the most adored king of Egypt; he was revered as not merely a ruler but also a divine guardian.

But, of course, not everyone looked up to him. Set, in particular, was jealous of his brother, Osiris. The god of chaos was often associated with the wild desert winds and storms. He was equally revered and feared for the chaos he represented. Despite not being abandoned by the Egyptians (they also worshiped Set back then, as he embodied balance), Set wanted more. The god of chaos could not sit still while his brother continued to sit on the throne, bringing harmony and order to the world. He wished to sit on the throne himself so he could impose his own rule of unpredictability and strife.

To make his ambitions come true, Set devised a rather sinister plan to usurp the throne. He began crafting a chest that was so exquisite that it would tempt anyone who laid eyes upon it. It was made with only the best materials, including rare pieces of wood, gold, and precious stones. This masterpiece of craftsmanship was not meant to be a gift for his brother. It was specifically designed to ensnare Osiris.

The god of chaos organized a lavish banquet. He invited nearly the entire pantheon of gods and goddesses, along with several foreign monarchs. It was an unimaginable feast with plenty of food and beautiful decorations. Among the guests was none other than Osiris, who was oblivious to his brother's scheme. Without wasting too much time, Set brought out the beautiful wooden chest. Perhaps with a sinister smile on his face, the god of chaos proclaimed that the chest would be gifted to whomever it fit perfectly. Little did the guests know, but Set had already constructed the chest to fit only Osiris. One by one, the guests tried to fit into the chest, and no one succeeded in doing so.

Finally, it was Osiris's turn to lay down in the chest. He fit into it like a glove. This was the very moment Set had been waiting for. He sprang into action, closing the lid and sealing the chest shut. Some suggest that this was the precursor of Egyptian sarcophagi. Set's plan did not end there. He immediately took the chest containing his brother and cast it into the Nile.

The chest—or perhaps the coffin—was swept away for many days. It drifted along the Nile and finally out to sea, where it eventually reached the shores near Byblos. The coffin was left untouched, and as time passed, a great tamarisk tree grew around it as if it were protecting the chest and the remains of the mighty god inside it.

Since the tamarisk had a powerful god within it, the tree gave out a divine aura, attracting those who passed by. One of them was the king of Byblos. Perhaps sensing magic or a sense of divinity in the great tamarisk, the king ordered the tree to be cut down. He then commanded that its trunk (the part that contained Egypt's most revered god and king) be brought straight to his grand palace so that he could use it as a pillar to support the roof of his house.

With Osiris gone, the throne was vacant. Knowing that there was no obstacle in his way, Set proclaimed himself the new king of Egypt. His reign was a stark contrast to the golden era of Osiris. The kingdom had enjoyed prosperity. However, with Set wearing the crown, crops withered, and the people despaired. It was as if the desert expanded its reach. Violent storms broke out, sweeping through the kingdom and leaving destruction in its wake. Agriculture became a thing of the past with the absence of the river's annual inundation.

It is important to note that the tale of Set and Osiris is not merely a story of envy and betrayal. It is a narrative that reflects the timeless dance of opposing forces and a reminder of the eternal struggle that lies at the heart of existence. Although Set was often pictured as an antagonist, especially in the story of Osiris, the god actually held a more complex and nuanced role. Despite his association with chaos, storms, and the desert, Set was an essential figure in the pantheon since he played a crucial role in maintaining the balance of the universe.

Many thousands of years ago, Set was placed on the higher levels of the pantheon. He was revered by the Egyptians as one of the most powerful deities to exist. His worship could be seen especially prominent in Upper Egypt, particularly in the city of Naqada. His reverence lasted for centuries; Ramesses II, for instance, held the god of chaos in high regard. He was also seen as a patron of warriors due to his strength and fierceness. Pharaohs often invoked Set's power in warfare, seeking his aid in battles.

Rituals and ceremonies dedicated to Set were known for their intensity. Some agree that this reflected his forceful nature. These rituals often involved animal sacrifices, which were seen as a way to appease and honor the god. However, not all animals could be sacrificed in the

Set holding the ankh and the Was scepter.[10]

name of Set. Most of the time, the Egyptians would choose creatures that were associated with the god, such as pigs, donkeys, or hippopotami.

Temples dedicated to Set were once common, although they were not widespread in every city. The greatest example is the Temple of Set at Naqada. Unfortunately, much of this temple has been claimed by Mother Nature. However, many artifacts depicting Set, including statues and reliefs, have been unearthed in various archaeological sites across Egypt. These artifacts often portray Set in his animal form.

One of the most intriguing aspects of Set's representation in Egyptian art is the Set animal (sometimes known as the sha). This creature has a slender body and a squared head with a long snout. To untrained eyes, the creature may appear similar to a dog. However, these features are not attributable to any known animal, which clearly signifies the mysterious and unique nature of the god Set.

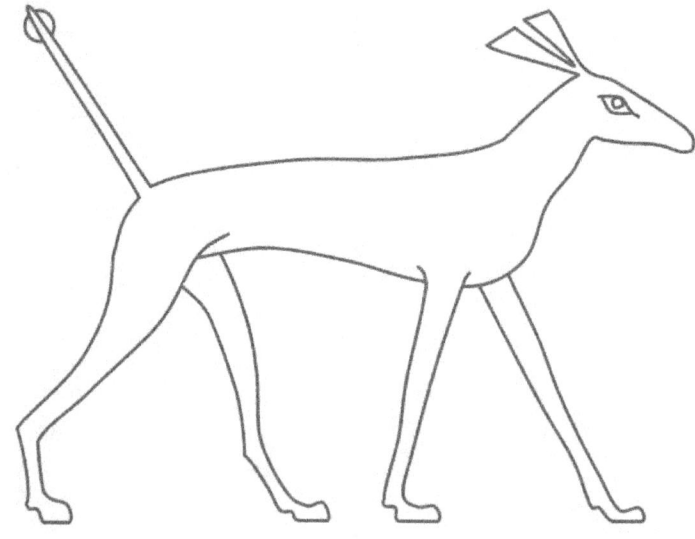

**A drawing of the Set animal or sha.**[11]

In the eyes of the ancient Greeks, Set's mysterious and formidable character found a parallel in their own mythology. They identified Set with Typhon, a monstrous serpentine giant and one of the deadliest creatures in Greek mythology.

In Greek mythology, Typhon was known as the father of all monsters. He was a fearsome figure of destruction and chaos. He was said to have the power to spew fire and challenge the might of Zeus, the king of the Greek gods. This image of Typhon is very similar to Set, who, in Egyptian mythology, was often seen as a figure of disruption and disorder. Both deities embodied the raw forces of nature and the untamed aspects of the world. Just as Typhon was essential in the Greek pantheon despite his fearsome nature, Set played a crucial role in Egyptian myths. The only difference, however, is that Typhon was a monstrous figure and never a symbol of balance. Set, on the other hand, had a crucial role in maintaining the balance of Ma'at (the Egyptian concept of balance and order) despite being seen as an adversary to gods like Osiris and Horus.

Apart from being highlighted as the main antagonist in the tale of Osiris, Set also starred in an episode involving Ra's fight against Apophis. Interestingly, Set was not associated with Ra at all initially. He was primarily associated with chaos, deserts, storms, and foreign lands. However, over time, as Egyptian religious beliefs evolved, Set's role in the mythology underwent significant changes. This shift is partly attributed to the political and social changes in Egypt, where a god's role was often reinterpreted to reflect the changing dynamics of power and beliefs.

The turning point for Set's role came during the Second Intermediate Period of Egypt. Historically, this was a time of great turmoil and foreign invasions. Set was associated with foreign lands, so he was initially viewed in a negative light. However, once the Egyptians successfully repelled these invasions, Set began to be seen more as a defender against external chaos rather than a bringer of it. This reimagining of Set's role paved the way for his portrayal as a protector.

And so, a myth that pictured Set as a mighty protector emerged. In this story, he could be seen defending Ra aboard the sun god's barque. Set was thought to have possessed formidable strength and ferocity, and many Egyptians held on to the belief that he was one of the few gods who could stand against Apophis. He was often depicted standing at the prow of Ra's boat, fiercely fighting off the serpent with his spear. Some sources claim there were times when Apophis successfully hypnotized Ra and the other gods present on the barque. Only Set managed to resist the cobra's magic, allowing him to defeat Apophis with his divine spear. This role highlights a more positive aspect of Set's character. By protecting Ra, Set ensured the continuation of the cycle of day and night, which was crucial for life on Earth and in the underworld.

Set thrusting his spear into Apophis, ensuring Ra's protection.[12]

## Osiris, a God Revered in Both Life and Death

Following the success of Set's brutal scheme, Osiris was left with no choice but to go through a fate worse than death. Not only was he torn from the throne of Egypt, but he was also trapped inside the chest for a very long time. Eventually, he suffocated and died. Yet, his journey was far from being over. His remains would not stay in the grand palace of the Byblos king forever. Isis, Osiris's loyal wife, although in mourning, would embark on a quest to find and resurrect her beloved husband—a tale we will explore in more detail later on.

Ultimately, Isis succeeded in retrieving Osiris and resurrected him. However, fate had already been written; the living world had to bid farewell to Osiris. To follow his destiny, Osiris had to resign from his title as the beloved king of Egypt and transition to become the god of the underworld. True, his absence was felt in the world of the living, but the realm of the dead saw the arrival of a just and wise king who would remain there for eternity, adjudicating over the souls of the departed.

**Wall painting in the tomb of Pharaoh Horemheb featuring Osiris (seated), Anubis, and Horus.**[13]

In his new role, Osiris acted as a steward to the souls of the deceased. Because of his association with the underworld, he was often depicted as a mummified king. His skin was green, which represented vegetation and rebirth, while his pharaoh's beard was associated with royalty. He was also often depicted with a crook and a flail crossed over his chest. The crook signified kingship, guidance, and protection, similar to a shepherd's care for his flock, and the flail represented authority, discipline, and fertility.

The mythology surrounding Osiris influenced Egyptian burial practices. His story encouraged the belief in an afterlife, a realm where justice and harmony prevailed under his wise rule, which led to the development of elaborate burial rituals, with the deceased being equipped with spells and items necessary for a safe journey to the afterlife. The Book of the Dead, a collection of spells and instructions, was often placed in tombs to guide the deceased through the Duat (the Egyptian underworld) and into the presence of Osiris.

Osiris was revered as the original archetype of kingship. The pharaohs of Egypt were seen as earthly embodiments of Horus, the falcon-headed god and son of Osiris. However, upon their death, the pharaoh's association transitioned from Horus to Osiris. In death, they were believed to have become Osiris himself. This belief was central to Egyptian funerary practices, as the mummification process and burial rituals were designed to mirror what Osiris went through. The pharaohs were mummified to resemble the god with the intention of being reborn in the afterlife, just as Osiris was resurrected by Isis.

A depiction of Osiris judging the dead in the Hall of Judgment from the Book of the Dead.¹⁴

The worship of Osiris was widespread. His cult centers could be seen dotted throughout Egypt. The most significant of these was Abydos, where the Osireion, a large temple complex dedicated to him, became a major pilgrimage site. Here, the faithful gathered to celebrate the mysteries of Osiris, rituals that commemorated his death and resurrection. Another important cult center was at Busiris in the Nile Delta. Here, he was worshiped as the lord of the underworld and the judge of the dead.

It is not surprising that Osiris's influence extended beyond religious practices. He became an important part of the daily lives of ancient Egyptians. When he was alive, Osiris was seen as a just and benevolent ruler. He was considered an ideal king who had brought civilization to Egypt. His death and resurrection, on the other hand, were seen as the ultimate acts of sacrifice for the benefit of all mankind. This narrative of a god-king who triumphs over betrayal and death resonated deeply with the Egyptian people, offering them hope and comfort in the face of their own mortality.

His relationship with other deities, especially his wife Isis and his son Horus, further enriched the mythology surrounding him. Isis's devotion to resurrect Osiris and Horus's quest to avenge his father's death showed the importance of familial loyalty and divine justice.

Osiris (middle) flanked by his son, Horus (left), and his wife, Isis (right).[15]

Osiris was honored in many festivals and celebrations. The most popular of all was the Khoiak festival. During this festival, the ancient Egyptians would engage in a series of rituals that culminated in the planting of "Osiris beds," which were filled with soil and barley. This was to symbolize the resurrection of life from the dead earth. Scholars suggest that this ritualistic planting was a physical manifestation of the Egyptians' deep connection with agriculture and their belief in the cyclical nature of life, death, and rebirth, as personified by Osiris.

# Chapter 4: Love and Magic: Isis

In 51 BCE, Cleopatra rose to the throne of Egypt. She was of Macedonian origins, yet the queen succeeded in gaining the favor of the majority of her subjects. Cleopatra was the only Ptolemaic pharaoh who could speak Egyptian despite her veins not carrying any Egyptian blood. Interestingly, Egyptian and Greek were not the only languages she was fluent in; Cleopatra could speak at least nine different languages. Perhaps this fluency in different tongues was one of the factors that contributed to her diplomatic prowess.

As a pharaoh, Cleopatra knew she had to appear extravagant. It was common for her to appear in public dressed in a kalasiris. This simple yet elegant sheath dress was a staple of Egyptian fashion at that time. Cleopatra was also said to have worn exquisite jewelry and precious stones. On her head, she would have sported a diadem. However, it was during religious ceremonies that Cleopatra's image caught the attention of many.

Typically, during these sacred occasions, the pharaoh would transform her image into that of the goddess Isis. She would wear a different kind of sheath dress that was likely more extravagant than usual. It is plausible that her ceremonial dresses were made of fine, pleated linen. They were also dyed in colors that symbolized divinity and royalty. Over her dress, the queen might have worn the Usekh, a type of collar or necklace usually worn only by Egyptian royals and elites. Even their goddesses were often depicted wearing one. Her other jewelry included bracelets and anklets, each bearing motifs associated with Isis, such as the scarab, lotus flower, or the sun disk cradled between the horns of a cow. The latter represented another goddess, Hathor, who was closely linked to Isis.

The vulture crown.[16]

Instead of a simple diadem, Cleopatra wore ceremonial headgear, such as the vulture crown. Just as the name suggests, the crown was in the shape of a vulture, with both of its wings hanging down on both sides. Apart from its unique shape, the crown also featured hundreds of gemstones, from lapis lazuli to turquoise. Other sources also suggest that the queen once appeared before her subjects wearing a headdress resembling a throne or a seat, a symbol of the goddess Isis and royalty. According to tradition, Isis was a personification of the throne.

To the ancient Egyptians, Cleopatra was more than just a ruler. She was thought to be the living manifestation of Isis, who was the goddess of motherhood, magic, and healing. The queen herself embraced this view. She knew it was important to align herself with the core values of Egyptian society, which included devotion, loyalty, and the sanctity of family.

So, what role did Isis exactly play in Egyptian mythology, and why was the goddess held in such high regard, especially by women? The answer is simple: Isis was considered the divine mother of the pharaoh. Also known in Egyptian as Aset or Eset, Isis was one of the most important beings in the Heliopolitan creation myth. She was one of the offspring of Geb (the god of the earth) and Nut (the sky goddess). Her siblings were Osiris, Set, and Nephthys. With Osiris, who was also her husband, the two had a child named Horus (the falcon-headed god), who later became the divine model of kingship itself.

Isis as depicted in the tomb of Seti I, 1360 BCE.[17]

As a goddess of magic, she was believed to possess profound and secret knowledge, giving her power over all beings. Her power even surpassed that of Ra, the chief god. Her magical abilities were most famously depicted in the story of Osiris's resurrection, where she used her powers to reassemble his body and bring him back to life.

Isis was also known as the goddess of magic. She was said to have possessed all knowledge in the universe, giving her power over all beings. Her power surpassed even that of Ra, the god of the sun. Her magical abilities could be seen clearly in the story of Osiris's resurrection. Isis was also revered as the goddess of motherhood and fertility. Her devotion to Osiris and Horus is still remembered as the ideal of maternal love and dedication. Being a healer, ancient Egyptians often invoked her name for protection and the healing of illnesses.

Similar to other important deities of the Egyptian pantheon, like Ra, Osiris, and Horus, Isis had many temples built in her honor. The most significant of all was the Philae Temple Complex. Currently located on Agilkia Island near Aswan (the temple complex was initially built on Philae Island until it was relocated in the 20th century CE due to a flood). This temple was also the center of her cult. Complete with grand pylons and awe-inspiring colonnades, the temple complex impressed many with its towering gateways and intricate reliefs depicting scenes of the goddess and her divine family. Inside the temple were more hieroglyphs that told the stories of her myths and her strong love for Osiris. One could also find a sanctuary located at the center of the temple. This sacred room was where a statue of Isis was kept. Most of the time, this room was dimly lit. Religious ceremonies once took place there. Ancient Egyptians would flock to the temple to make offerings and pray to receive the goddess's blessings.

Temple of Isis in Philae, Aswan, Egypt.[18]

Isis's influence was not only limited to Egypt. The goddess also found a place within Roman culture and religion. Initially, the worship of Isis was viewed with skepticism in the Eternal City. This was mostly due to its foreign origins. However, as time passed, the cult of Isis gained popularity, especially among the commoners. Many were attracted to Isis because of the universal themes in her stories. The stories of resurrection, healing, and protection resonated deeply with the Roman populace. Eventually, the Eternal City accepted her worship more openly to the point where festivals were held in honor of the goddess. One of them was known as the Navigium Isidis, which celebrated the start of the sailing season.

It is safe to assume that the integration of Isis into Roman culture had to do with Cleopatra, who had significant influence over the Romans after her relationships with Julius Caesar and Mark Antony. Temples and statues of Isis began to dot Roman cities. The Romans were known for assimilating deities from other cultures, so it is not a surprise that Isis was woven into their religious beliefs. Her image, however, went through some changes; this modification was done to align her more with Roman sensibilities. In the Eternal City, it was more common to see her depicted in Roman garb and have attributes that made her more relatable to the Roman populace.

Later on, Isis became closely associated with Venus (Aphrodite in Greek mythology), who was known as the Roman goddess of love and beauty. This association largely stemmed from the similar attributes both deities shared, such as femininity, motherhood, and a strong connection to nature and fertility. Both goddesses were also seen as patrons of sailors and protectors of the seas.

However, it is important to note that while there were similarities, Isis and Aphrodite/Venus remained distinct entities within their respective mythologies. Isis's role within the Egyptian pantheon was deeply rooted in themes of magic, resurrection, and familial devotion, which were not primary attributes of Aphrodite/Venus. Nonetheless, the blending of these goddesses in the Roman period highlights the cultural exchanges and religious syncretism that occurred in the ancient world.

### The Legend of How Isis Tricked the Sun God, Ra

According to legend, Isis sought to gain the same power as Ra, the mightiest god of the Egyptian pantheon. True, Ra was wise and powerful, but his old age was slowly catching up to him. Legend has it that the sun god was beginning to weaken--though not entirely. His saliva was said to have dribbled as he spoke, and he no longer had the same control over the vast world as he had in his prime. This was the very opportunity that Isis was patiently waiting for.

The goddess aimed not to seize power from the sun god but rather to expand her abilities. She knew that Ra's power was in his secret name, a name that held the essence of his true being and the source of his divine power. However, this name was a closely guarded secret known only to Ra himself. Determined to learn this name, Isis devised a plan. She collected the saliva that dribbled from Ra's mouth as he slept and mixed it with earth, creating a venomous snake.

This snake was then placed on Ra's path. When Ra walked by, the snake bit him, injecting its potent venom. The pain was immediate and intense, but no god or magician could relieve Ra's suffering since the poison was of divine creation.

In her guise as a healer, Isis approached Ra. She offered to cure him but only on the condition that he reveal his secret name to her. Ra was in unbearable agony, but he resisted at first, offering her wealth and power instead, but none of these could sway Isis. She knew that only his secret name would give her the power she desired.

Eventually, weakened by pain and realizing he had no other option, Ra consented. He whispered his secret name to Isis, which granted her an immense power that rivaled his own. With this knowledge, Isis healed Ra of the snake's venom, but from that moment forward, she held a portion of his power, elevating her status among the gods.

### Divine Family Drama

When news of her husband's sudden death reached her, Isis was immediately overwhelmed with grief and sadness. Yes, her heart ached because she had lost her husband, but she was also in deep sorrow knowing that the world had been plunged into chaos and turmoil under Set. Isis could not sit and do nothing while her brother, Set, ruled over Egypt. The goddess knew she had to do everything she could to restore balance, and the first step to achieving that was to find Osiris's body.

The search was undeniably hard. Isis scoured Egypt day and night. After days, maybe weeks or months, of relentless searching, Isis's efforts were rewarded. She met a few children who saw a peculiar wooden chest floating in the direction of Byblos. And so, disguised as an old woman, Isis made her way to the city. The story says that the goddess managed to impress the queen of Byblos so much that she eventually entrusted the disguised Isis with the care of her son.

However, instead of nursing the Byblos prince as one normally would, Isis performed a secret ritual every night. She bathed the young prince in fire, which eventually purged him of his mortal constraints. While doing this, Isis was also said to have transformed into a swallow, flying around the palace in search of the pillar that held her husband. Eventually, the queen of Byblos stumbled upon the scene, flames dancing around the young prince. Horrified by the sight of her own son hugged by burning fire, the queen screamed as loud as she could. Perhaps startled by the scream and not wanting to cause further commotion, Isis quickly reverted to her true form. Revealing herself as a goddess and seizing the opportunity, Isis told her story and begged for the pillar that contained Osiris.

It was hard to deny a god, especially one that was well respected. With the pillar now in her possession, Isis carefully extracted the chest. After opening it, the goddess burst into tears. Her husband was lying still, his body cold. Knowing the danger that lingered if Set ever knew of her discovery, Isis hid the body in a marshland. She planned to perform the rituals that could resurrect Osiris.

Unfortunately for her, Set discovered Isis's actions. Overwhelmed with rage, Set was believed to have cut Osiris's body into fourteen pieces before scattering them all over Egypt. This act of desecration was a severe blow to Isis's hopes, but her resolve did not waver. The following morning, finding Osiris's body gone, Isis went on another journey. Thankfully, she was not alone in this quest. Nephthys, the wife of Set, helped out in the search effort and greatly aided Isis. Nephthys was, after all, a protector of the dead. She symbolized the death experience, just as Isis represented the experience of birth. So, together, the two goddesses combined their powers and wisdom in their quest to restore balance.

The task was daunting, but Isis was never known to back down. She eventually found the first piece of her dismembered husband, followed by the second, the third, and so on. With each discovery, Isis's determination grew. She eventually succeeded in retrieving all the pieces of her husband except for one, his penis, which had been eaten by a type of fish known as Oxyrhynchus (also known as Medjed). This was the reason why ancient Egyptians were prohibited from eating this fish.

With the thirteen pieces of Osiris gathered in one place, Isis and a few other gods, including Nephthys, Thoth, and Anubis, then began the task of reassembling —or sewing—Osiris's remains. Night after night, they worked, and when the body was whole again, they wrapped it in linen, creating the first mummy. Isis then worked on her magic. Only when the sky turned dark could the goddess resurrect Osiris and embrace him once more. It was believed that this was also the time that the two conceived their son, Horus.

Unfortunately, this act of resurrection was not able to hold Osiris in the living world for too long. The god embraced Isis once more and expressed his gratitude for her loyalty. However, he also told her that it was not his destiny to live in the same world as hers. Without all fourteen pieces of himself, Osiris was not allowed to live in the mortal realm. He was not to rule the living; instead, he would become the king of the afterlife. He was meant to remain in the Du'at (the world of the dead), where his main responsibility was to judge the souls of the departed.

Isis was clearly devastated. Osiris calmed his wife and reassured her that their legacy was not over yet. Osiris told her of a prophecy that would bring honor back to their family. Osiris claimed that their son, Horus, would defeat Set and rise as the great protector of the Egyptians. Horus would be the one to avenge Osiris, restore order, and reintroduce peace once more to Egypt after claiming the throne from Set. Isis was relieved by this, and she began accepting the fact that her husband had to move on.

Osiris's departure to the Du'at marked the beginning of his transition from a god and king of the living to the lord of the underworld. Isis, on the other hand, turned her focus on raising and protecting their son, Horus. Yet, some claimed the goddess never stopped missing her husband. She would cry every year, her tears turning into the annual flood that took place across Egypt. However, despite missing her husband, Isis never failed to ensure her son's safety. The goddess was well aware that she must do everything in her power to ensure Horus's rightful place in the world. She had to keep her eyes open all the time since Horus's path was always filled with danger. His uncle, Set, knew no rest; he posed a constant threat to both Horus and Isis. Isis used her wisdom and magical skills to protect Horus until he was finally ready to challenge Set and reclaim the crown.

### Isis and the Status of Women in Ancient Egypt

Isis was a major goddess in Egyptian mythology. She had a strong influence on the status and role of women in ancient Egypt. She was often portrayed as a devoted wife, a loving mother, and a powerful goddess—all qualities that gave women a positive role model to look up to.

In contrast to women from other ancient civilizations, women in ancient Egypt enjoyed more rights and higher status. Not only could they own property and run businesses, but Egyptian women were allowed to initiate divorce. The respect people had for Isis might have helped women gain more respect in everyday life.

The worship of Isis also provided women with a divine role model. Women were given a chance to devote themselves fully to the heavens. Some served as priestesses in temples built in honor of the goddess. They were also in charge of performing rituals and ceremonies. This way, women in Egypt were given a position of respect within their communities. Although the influence of Isis spread into the Roman world, her worship did not change the status of Roman women; the structure of Roman society remained mostly the same.

Beyond the ancient world, the legacy of Isis continues to resonate with people, finding relevance and undergoing reinterpretation in the modern era, notably within contemporary feminist discourse. In feminist perspectives, Isis is often viewed as an early embodiment of the empowered woman. Her narrative, characterized by resilience, intelligence, and the ability to protect and advocate for her family, parallels modern ideas about female empowerment and self-determination. The story of Isis—her journey to reclaim Osiris's body and her instrumental role in securing Horus's future—mirrors contemporary narratives where women actively shape their destiny and advocate for themselves and their loved ones. The influence of Isis also permeates modern culture, as she is often revisited in literature, art, and media. She is typically portrayed as a figure of wisdom, nurturing, and protection, underscoring her lasting impact across different cultures and time periods. Although no longer worshiped, the enduring legacy of Isis in the modern world serves as a source of inspiration and reflection in discussions about femininity, power, and resilience.

# Chapter 5: The God of Mummification: Anubis

In ancient Egypt, belief in the afterlife reigned supreme. The art of mummification was more than just a mere ritual; it was seen as a bridge to eternity. The embalmer stood in a chamber filled with the aroma of incense and the weight of tradition. Surrounded by an array of tools forged from the finest bronze and iron, he prepared to embark on the meticulous journey of preservation. Under the watchful eyes of painted deities, the embalmer surveyed the room around him. The chamber was lined with jars of oils and spices, and in the center of the room lay the body. Before him was a variety of sharp flint knives, each serving its own unique purpose in the ritual. The deceased was a nobleman adorned in lavish garments, though they had to be removed. The embalmer began his work with ceremonial prayers, seeking the protection of the gods before he made the first incision. Once he finished praying to the gods, the embalmer made a small yet precise cut in the lower left abdomen.

He was not alone in this process. The embalmer was also accompanied by his assistants, who observed his delicate hands working on the operation. To ensure the mummification process went smoothly, he had to remove each organ inside the body. However, these organs were not to be discarded; each of them held its own significance. The first to be extracted was the intestines. This particular organ was believed to be the seat of turmoil. Therefore, it needed special attention. If left unattended or decayed, the soul of the deceased would face unrest in the afterlife.

Once successfully extracted in one piece, the intestines were carefully dropped into a large pottery bowl. Then, the bowl was filled with natron. This special type of preservative agent was found only in the dry lake beds to the northwest of Thebes. Natron was essential in the process of mummification; without it, the embalmer would not be able to prevent decomposition.

After the intestines, the embalmer moved on to remove the stomach, liver, and lungs. These organs were also treated gently. They were first cleaned before going through the process of preservation. The liver was a symbol of strength and vitality, but there is no clear evidence in surviving Egyptian texts that explains what specific symbolic meanings the other two organs held.

Only the heart was left inside the body, as this organ was said to have been the center of a person's being. According to traditional Egyptian beliefs, the heart encompassed a person's physical essence, thoughts, and feelings. It was highly important to keep it intact during the mummification process. However, ensuring the heart remained unscathed was not an easy task, even for the most experienced embalmer. The heart was located close to the lungs, so there was always the possibility of the embalmer accidentally hurting the organ as he removed the lungs.

It was only when the upper torso was emptied of its internal organs that the embalmer would move on to the next step. Using palm wine, he would clean the cavities, ensuring no blood could be seen and that no foul scent lingered in the air.

He then turned his attention back to the organs that he had carefully extracted. They were wrapped in linen and placed safely in canopic jars. These jars were not merely containers. Each was carved out of limestone and adorned with intricate hieroglyphs. These vessels were then closed off using different lids bearing the faces of the four sons of Horus. The stomach was sealed with a lid bearing an image of the jackal-headed god Duamutef, and the lungs were guarded by Hapi, which was depicted with the head of a baboon. Imsety, who had a human head, watched over the liver, and Qebehsenuef, with the head of a falcon, kept the intestines safe. These guardians ensured that the organs would be reunited with the body in the afterlife.

Animal-headed canopic jars from the Twenty-sixth Dynasty (664–525 BCE).[19]

The brain was considered by ancient Egyptians to be inconsequential. The embalmer would use a long, slender iron, which he carefully inserted through the nostrils. He would gently shove it in until he could feel the soft, delicate brain tissue. With skilled twists and turns, he fragmented the brain, with his assistant holding the head steady during the entire process. It is safe to assume that this task required both precision and patience. After multiple gentle prods, the brain would eventually turn into a thick, viscous liquid. Then, the embalmer and his assistants flipped the corpse over. They would slap the back of the skull, allowing the liquid to flow out through the dead person's nasal passage. Once the skull was free from even the tiniest bits of the brain, the embalmer would then meticulously clean the cranial cavity and prepare the skull for its eternal rest.

With the organs and brain finally removed, the body was now ready for desiccation. Again, natron, a naturally occurring salt, was the embalmer's main tool in this stage. The body was thoroughly cleaned and then covered inside and out with heaps of natron. The corpse, now seen as a vessel for the soul's journey, was left in a state of rest, completely submerged in natron. This period of desiccation lasted for forty days, during which the body slowly transformed. The natron absorbed all moisture, leaving the skin dry and leathery, leaving it perfectly preserved for the next stage.

After the natron treatment, the body was carefully unwrapped from its salty cocoon. It was cleansed once more, this time with oils and fragrances, in preparation for its final adornment. The wrapping of the body was considered a sacred act, so it was common for rituals and prayers to be performed. Then, the embalmer began to enfold the body in hundreds of yards of linen. As the layers of linen accumulated, the embalmer recited prayers. He believed each wrap was a step closer to immortality. Amulets and charms were also placed between the folds, ensuring protection and guidance in the underworld.

Once that was done, the embalmer placed a mask over the wrapped head of the mummy. The design and quality of these masks differed based on the deceased's social standing. Wealthy individuals often had elaborate masks adorned with gold and detailed with fine paint. Those from less affluent backgrounds typically had simpler masks featuring more basic designs without elaborate decorations. The situation was similar with amulets. The wealthy were buried with numerous amulets crafted from precious stones, while those with fewer resources might have only a handful of amulets made from less expensive materials.

A mummy mask.[30]

The process of mummification took a total of seventy days to complete. Only then would the mummy be prepared for its burial in a tomb, which had been designed and constructed in advance. These burials were typically accompanied by elaborate rituals intended to prepare the deceased for their journey into the next life. Mummies were often placed inside a sarcophagus, which was then placed in the burial chamber of the tomb. Once everything was in place, the entrance to the tomb was sealed, marking the moment when the soul of the departed began its journey to the afterlife.

Of course, such elaborate mummification was not done on everyone. Interestingly, recent studies found that there were no standardized methods of mummification across all the regions of Egypt. The less wealthy, for instance, were possibly mummified with simpler methods. More often than not, their organs were not removed. Instead, embalmers would pour juniper oil into the body cavity to dissolve the organs. Their bodies were also not wrapped intricately in linen but rather buried in the hot desert, which naturally dried them out and eventually preserved them.

**Anubis, the Guide of the Dead**

With the mummy securely placed within the sarcophagus and the tomb's entrance sealed, a profound transformation occurred. With the physical rites completed, the soul of the departed embarked on its journey into the realm of the afterlife.

In this realm of shadows, the deceased would be greeted by Anubis, the jackal-headed god. Although his role in ancient Egyptian mythology, especially in death and funerary rites, was important, Anubis had a rather inconsistent origin. Some sources claim Anubis was the son of Ra and was crowned as the god of the dead. In this early depiction, he was seen as the sole ruler of the afterlife. His connection to Ra further added a celestial aspect to his dominion, intertwining the cycles of life and death with the daily journey of the sun across the sky.

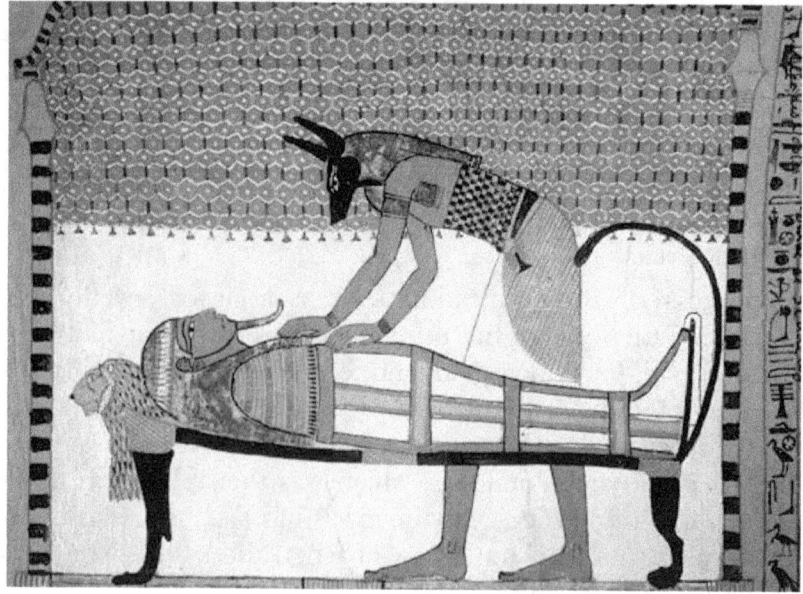

Anubis tending to a mummy.[31]

However, with the rise of Osiris's cult, this version of the story where Anubis was seen as the sole ruler of the underworld underwent a significant shift. The title of the king of the underworld was given to Osiris instead. Therefore, Anubis was no longer considered the primary ruler of the deceased. His role evolved, and he became known as the god of funerary rites and the guardian of the dead. Anubis became more closely related to the process of mummification and the protection of graves and cemeteries.

Then, by 2000 BCE, another origin story emerged that linked Anubis to Nephthys. Nephthys, who was married to Set, found herself drawn to Osiris. Perhaps driven by both lust and longing, Nephthys was said to have disguised herself as the goddess Isis and seduced Osiris. Through this union, Anubis was born. However, Nephthys was well aware of the wrath and retribution that would dawn upon her should Set ever discover her affair with Osiris. So, the goddess chose to make a heart-wrenching decision. She left the newborn Anubis in a desolate area, abandoning him so that she could conceal evidence of her infidelity. Set eventually discovered this affair, which further fueled his desire to end Osiris.

As for Anubis, Isis discovered him. The goddess knew of the affair between Osiris and Nephthys, but as the goddess of motherhood and compassion, she did not have the heart to abandon Anubis. She took the infant into her care, raising him as her own. By doing so, she forged a bond of deep loyalty and gratitude in him. Perhaps as a gesture of gratitude, Anubis became her most loyal ally and supporter. This relationship was most prominently displayed in the myth of Osiris's resurrection.

His mysterious origins aside, we can safely assume that Anubis offered the dead solace in their journey through the afterlife. In Egyptian mythology, he was revered for his strength, wisdom, fairness, and knowledge of the mystical arts. He stood as the sentinel of the afterlife and a protector of the dead, guiding them through their journey to eternity.

The ancient Egyptian Book of the Dead was a sacred text that served as a guide, offering spells, prayers, and instructions to the deceased. The soul, accompanied by Anubis, embarked on a perilous path through this mystical domain, facing challenges that tested its worthiness for the afterlife.

This journey involved traversing through dark waters, confronting fearsome creatures, and navigating through gates guarded by formidable beings. Each step of the way, the soul encountered various gods and demons who presented their own riddles and tasks. These trials were essential since they purified the soul and prepared it for the ultimate judgment.

Anubis provided guidance and protection. He was the beacon in the darkness and the steady hand in moments of uncertainty. His knowledge of the underworld was unparalleled, making him the ideal shepherd for souls in their most vulnerable state.

Anubis was not just a passive escort. He actively engaged with the soul, offering wisdom and comfort. His presence was a constant reminder of the divine order and the righteousness of the path they walked. He was particularly present at critical junctures of the journey where the soul's fate hung in the balance. His guidance was crucial, for without it, the soul could easily lose its way, falling prey to the perils of the underworld. Anubis's main role was to ensure that each soul had a fair chance to reach its final destination, the Hall of Ma'at, where the ultimate judgment awaited it.

The climax of this journey was the Weighing of the Heart ceremony. In the presence of Osiris and a panel of judges, the soul's heart was placed on a scale opposite the feather of Ma'at, which symbolized truth and justice. Anubis, the impartial arbiter, oversaw this ceremony with a stern but fair gaze. He ensured that the scales were balanced. The heart represented the deeds the soul had committed throughout its life. A heart lighter or equal in weight to the feather signified a life lived with integrity and truth, granting the soul passage to the Field of Reeds, a place of eternal peace and pleasure.

A heart heavier than the feather would be burdened by wrongdoing and sin. This soul faced a dire fate. It was devoured by Ammit, the devourer of souls, condemning the soul to oblivion. The Weighing of the Heart ceremony was the ultimate test of a soul's purity and righteousness.

In the post-Late Period of ancient Egypt, spanning from 664 to 30 BCE, Anubis again underwent another transformation, adding a new dimension to his already complex character. During this era, Anubis was still revered as the god of funerary rites and the guardian of the dead, but he also became closely associated with necromancy. This aspect of

Anubis highlights the Egyptians' deepening exploration into the mysteries of life, death, and the hereafter.

Anubis weighing the heart of the dead.[22]

Necromancy, the practice of communicating with the dead to predict the future or uncover hidden knowledge, became a part of certain religious and magical practices in Egypt. Anubis, with his intimate connection to the underworld and the afterlife, was naturally invoked in these rituals. He was seen as a powerful intermediary, a bridge between the living and the spirits of the deceased, as well as other deities who dwelled in the nether realm.

Demotic spells, written in the common script of the time, were often used to call upon Anubis in these necromantic practices. These spells were intricate and required a deep understanding of the rituals and language that were believed to hold sway in the supernatural world. Practitioners would perform elaborate ceremonies that often involved offerings, recitations, and specific gestures to invoke Anubis.

Upon his invocation, Anubis was believed to traverse the boundaries between the worlds. As a guide and protector in the underworld, he had unique access to spirits and gods who resided there. Those practicing necromancy would ask Anubis to fetch these spirits or gods since they sought their counsel or assistance. This could involve asking questions about the future, seeking guidance for important decisions, or even trying to gain knowledge about secret matters.

Anubis's portrayal as a jackal-headed god was itself steeped in symbolism. The jackal, an animal often seen around cemeteries, was associated with death and decay yet also with protection and guidance. Anubis's visage embodied these dual aspects, reflecting his role in guarding the dead and guiding them through the afterlife. Anubis was often shown holding the ankh, the symbol of life, and the scepter, which represented power and authority. These symbols highlighted his role as a giver of life in the afterlife and a deity capable of navigating the underworld.

**Anubis vs Set**

Osiris's death was felt by many, including the sun god Ra. In fact, Ra was the one who specifically requested that Anubis assist Isis in resurrecting Osiris. Since Anubis was extremely loyal to Isis, he did not hesitate to help. The resurrection process was said to have begun with the mummification of Osiris, which Anubis oversaw to ensure every phase was perfectly done. This was the very first time the Egyptians were introduced to mummification. Apart from preserving the body itself, the process also involved other important rituals. Among these was the Opening of the Mouth ceremony, a rite designed to ensure that Osiris could see, hear, breathe, and eat in the afterlife, effectively restoring his senses.

Of course, Anubis and the other gods were not free from obstacles. During the process, they had to face the schemes of Set, who was always watching their movements. When the god of chaos learned of the efforts to resurrect Osiris, he made haste to foil them. His chance came when Anubis had his hands full one day while working on embalming Osiris. At night, the god of embalming would leave the webet, the place where the embalming work took place, leaving Osiris's body alone with the guards. Seizing the opportunity, Set transformed himself into Anubis. He managed to convince the guards, allowing him to enter the webet and steal Osiris's body.

This theft was discovered by Anubis himself. Without wasting any time, he chased after the deceitful god of chaos. He knew he had to retrieve the body of Osiris. Set, realizing that Anubis was pursuing him, morphed into a bull. He confronted Anubis in this form, but the jackal-headed god proved to be stronger. Some sources say that Anubis succeeded in capturing and imprisoning Set, though this imprisonment was only for a short while.

This was not the last time the two gods would confront each other. Set transformed into a panther in order to steal the remains of Osiris again. However, Anubis had learned his lesson; ever since the first encounter, he had his eyes wide open for trouble. He knew Set would stop at nothing just so he could secure the throne for himself. Upon uncovering Set's plan, Anubis succeeded in capturing Set in his panther form. This time around, he branded him hundreds of times with a hot iron. This mythological tale is often cited as the reason why leopards have spots.

On the other hand, another account from a Ptolemaic papyrus known as Jumilhac tells us a different end. According to this version, Anubis was said to have skinned Set while he was in his leopard form. The jackal-headed god then wore his pelt as a trophy. Egyptologists and scholars view this as a symbol of Anubis's dominion over chaos and evil. This imagery was so powerful that it influenced Egyptian religious practices. Following the spread of this myth, priests began wearing leopard pelts as a symbol of their connection to Anubis and their role in maintaining order over chaos.

In modern times, Anubis is often portrayed as a malevolent deity, a figure shrouded in the darkness of death and mystery. This depiction, however, stands in stark contrast to the reverence and respect he commanded in ancient Egyptian culture. To the Egyptians, Anubis was not a symbol of fear or evil; instead, he was a revered guardian and guide, an essential figure in their spiritual and religious life.

# Chapter 6: The Guardians of Order: Thoth and Ma'at

There was once a man who lived in Memphis. He did not know it yet, but he was just hours away from experiencing a life-changing event. Unlike many other Egyptians of his time, the man had never experienced poverty. He was born into a well-off family and seldom went through hardship. Yet, he had a strange addiction. The man had a habit of taking things that did not belong to him. Of course, he was not a thief by career. The man simply loved the thrill of stealing.

One day, the man stole a piece of jewelry from an unsuspecting merchant. He had been eyeing it for days, and finally, fueled by both greed and the lust for a fortune not his own, he snatched it and calmly walked away. Later on, as the man passed through the winding streets lined with sandstone houses and lively market stalls, his path inadvertently led him past a temple. Here, an image of a certain goddess caught his attention. It was a relief of Ma'at, the goddess whose very essence was the embodiment of truth and justice. Familiar to all Egyptians, her presence reminded them of the moral and cosmic order. However, the sight of Ma'at did not stir remorse in the man's heart. He continued walking home without feeling even the slightest hint of regret in his heart.

The goddess Ma'at adorning the feather of truth.[28]

As night fell, he was sitting alone, admiring the stolen jewelry. It was so intricately made that the moment its facets caught the light, the room was immediately filled with a dance of shadows and radiance. The man smiled. He saw the jewel as something more than just a trinket. He viewed it as a symbol of his skill and audacity. Satisfied with his work for the day, the man placed the jewelry aside and fell asleep.

Suddenly, the familiar comfort of his bed gave way to an ethereal realm. He noticed that he was no longer in his safe home but in the mysterious and foreboding world of the Du'at, the Egyptian underworld.

The transition from the world of the living to the Du'at was a journey shrouded in mystery and ancient lore. For a pharaoh, the passage to the afterlife was almost like a ceremonial voyage. He would be assisted by spells, sacred rituals, and opulent tombs designed to ease his journey to the realm beyond. However, for ordinary Egyptians, like our unnamed man, the journey was very different. It would be a sudden and disorienting shift completely devoid of grandeur or guidance.

The man ventured deeper into this unknown world, eventually encountering the many guardians of the underworld. He could feel himself shivering before these divine entities. All of them had a rather formidable appearance. They were part animal, part god. These entities were the ones who upheld the realm's sacred laws. They stood before imposing gates, their eyes piercing through him as if peeling back the layers of his soul. With each step, he felt the weight of his stolen treasures like chains around his heart.

The realms he traversed were as terrifying as they were wondrous. He walked across a vast desert where he witnessed dozens of lost souls wandering around. Each of them was lamenting the many regrets of their lives. One spoke of his own greed, while another expressed her regret for abandoning the gods. The man also came across a dark river whose waters were deep and still. Although the man could not see any dangerous creatures lurking underneath the water, he could feel a sense of unease slowly crawling at the back of his neck.

His steps eventually brought him to the assembly of gods. Each of them was a representation of the virtues upheld by Ma'at. Among them were Osiris, the lord of the underworld; Anubis, the guardian of the scales; Thoth, the scribe of the gods; and others who embodied the divine aspects of justice, truth, and order. Before these deities, the man was compelled to recite the Negative Confession, a declaration of innocence against the forty-two sins of Ma'at's code. With each confession, he finally felt the weight of his past actions.

Ammit, the devourer of souls.[34]

Only upon completing this confession did the true test begin: the Weighing of the Heart. The man watched in silent horror as, one by one, the souls were judged. Some were granted passage to the Field of Reeds, a peaceful paradise. Others, whose hearts were filled with wrongdoing, faced the grim fate of being devoured by Ammit, the devourer of souls.

A depiction of Aaru or the Field of Reeds.[25]

When his turn came, the man could feel his heart racing. The scales were then set, and finally, his heart was placed on one side. The feather of Ma'at was placed on the other. Suddenly, the balance tipped. His heart was heavy with the weight of his misdeeds. The sight of this caused the man to lose his ability to breathe. His panic worsened the moment he saw Ammit's fearsome jaws get closer to his face. Then, everything went dark. He jolted awake.

He had never experienced such a nightmare before. Panting and drenched in his own sweat, the man lay still on his bed. He then recalled the time he saw an image of Ma'at carved at the temple he passed by the day before and realized the gods were indeed watching him. The terror of the dream left a lasting mark on him. He made a solemn vow to amend his ways. He resolved to align his life with the principles of truth and justice, ensuring that the nightmarish vision the gods had given him would never manifest into reality.

## The Concept of Ma'at in Ancient Egyptian Belief and as a Goddess

In the ancient Egyptian religion, Ma'at stood as the pillar of cosmic and societal order. She was more than just a goddess; she was also the embodiment of truth, balance, order, and justice. To the Egyptians, her influence could be felt in every aspect of existence, from the movement of the stars to the daily lives of mortals, be it the powerful pharaohs or common people. The concept of Ma'at was integral to maintaining harmony in the universe, as this harmony ensured the cyclical nature of life, from the flooding of the Nile to the transition of souls in the afterlife, continued to happen without disruption.

Ma'at was often depicted in human form as a woman with an ostrich feather (the feather of truth) atop her head. This feather represented the lightness and purity that truth brought to the soul. Temples dedicated to Ma'at were rare since her presence was more a part of the fabric of everyday life and state affairs rather than the focus of individual worship. Pharaohs, in particular, were seen as the earthly embodiments of Ma'at, and they were tasked with upholding her principles while ruling the kingdom.

Ma'at, as a goddess, was unique. She did not have the dramatic myths or narratives typical of other Egyptian deities. Instead, her power and influence were more abstract. As a symbol of moral and ethical righteousness, Ma'at was the touchstone against which all actions, both of deities and mortals, were measured. From the grandest temples to the humblest homes, her principles were the guiding force behind law, governance, and personal conduct. In religious ceremonies, offerings to Ma'at were common, as they symbolized the pharaoh's or an individual's commitment to upholding truth and balance in their reign and/or life.

The principles of Ma'at were not just religious doctrines but also a way of life. In societal terms, Ma'at represented the ideal state of affairs, where harmony prevailed and chaos was kept at bay. For the individual, living in accordance with Ma'at meant living a life of honesty, integrity, and moral righteousness. The concept of "living in Ma'at" was essential for one's personal well-being and prosperity.

## Thoth

While Ma'at stood as a guardian of the underworld and a beacon of truth and justice, she was not alone in her vigilant watch over the realms of the afterlife. Alongside her, another deity played a role of equal magnitude and mystery. This was Thoth. To the ancient Egyptian people, he was the god of wisdom, writing, and, sometimes, the moon.

Thoth's depiction in ancient Egyptian art is striking. This deity had the body of a man and the head of an ibis, his sharp beak a symbol of the precision of thought and language. In his hand, he often held a scribe's palette and stylus, ready to record the deeds of mortals and gods alike.

Thoth's name and origin are deeply rooted in the ancient Egyptian belief system. His name, *Dhwty* in the Egyptian language, means "he who is like the ibis." The ibis was an elegant bird and was commonly seen along the Nile. It was revered for its wisdom, a trait Thoth himself personified.

Legends about Thoth's birth vary. Some claim that he was self-created at the beginning of time, while others suggest he emerged from the lips of Ra, the sun god. This birth narrative positions Thoth not only as a divine being but also as an intrinsic part of the cosmic order, as his very existence is tied to the creation of the universe.

The worship of Thoth dates back to the predynastic period. He grew in prominence as the Egyptian civilization evolved. His main worship center was in Hermopolis, a city that became synonymous with Thoth's cult. The reverence for Thoth in Hermopolis was not just limited to grand temples and elaborate rituals. It also manifested in a more tangible, albeit peculiar, form. Pilgrims who came to the city, particularly during festivals, would often buy mummified ibises and baboons. These were votive offerings and were given in the hope of earning Thoth's favor.

Thoth, the Egyptian god of wisdom.[26]

Thoth's appeal transcended social hierarchies. While he was especially popular among the royals, who saw him as a divine arbitrator and the keeper of cosmic balance, commoners also showed their devotion to him. In an era when literacy was limited to a select few, Thoth represented the pinnacle of knowledge and wisdom. To venerate Thoth was to aspire to these esteemed qualities. His popularity reached its zenith during the New Kingdom. In this era, Thoth was not just a god to be feared or appeased; he was also seen as a symbol of enlightenment, guiding the Egyptians in both their worldly pursuits and their spiritual endeavors.

Thoth played a crucial role in the shadowy realm of the Du'at, the ancient Egyptian underworld. In the solemn chamber where the hearts of the deceased were weighed against the feather of Ma'at, Thoth stood among the other gods as the impartial scribe. It was his divine duty to record the proceedings, keeping meticulous accounts of each soul's life and actions. As the scales tipped to reveal the truth, Thoth chronicled the outcome.

Thoth's role in the Book of the Dead is particularly illustrative of his importance. He is often depicted before the scales, quill and palette in hand, ready to inscribe the verdict. This critical function elevated Thoth to the status of a deity embodying truth and integrity. The Egyptians revered him for this impartiality, often expressing a desire to live a life "straight and true like Thoth."

Beyond his duties in the Hall of Truth, Thoth's influence in the underworld extended to his abode, known as the Mansion of Thoth. This was a sanctuary for souls. The Mansion of Thoth was seen as a safe haven, a place where souls could find respite and protection. It was here that Thoth, with his boundless knowledge, bestowed magic spells upon the souls, empowering them to face and overcome the demons that lurked in the underworld seeking to impede their journey to paradise. These spells were powerful incantations imbued with the wisdom and authority of Thoth. They served as a shield against the terrors of the Du'at.

The lore of Thoth as the creator of knowledge casts him in an even more magnificent light. Thoth was credited with the creation and mastery of several branches of knowledge that shaped the spiritual and intellectual landscape of ancient Egypt.

Thoth was revered as the originator of law, laying down the foundation for order and justice in society. He was seen as the ultimate arbitrator whose wisdom was indispensable in resolving conflicts and maintaining balance. His influence extended to magic, where he was regarded as the supreme magician whose knowledge of spells and incantations was unmatched. This aspect of Thoth resonated deeply with the Egyptian belief in the power of words and rituals to influence the natural and supernatural worlds.

Thoth's contributions were no less significant in philosophy. He was thought to be the one who crafted the fabric of Egyptian religious and philosophical thought, providing insights into the mysteries of existence and the cosmos. Science, too, fell under Thoth's domain. He was the measurer of the earth and the counter of the stars, a deity whose wisdom understood the inner workings of the universe.

However, perhaps the most enduring of Thoth's creations was writing. The god was attributed with the invention of hieroglyphics, the sacred script that not only recorded the history and culture of ancient Egypt but was also believed to hold magical powers. The ancient Egyptians believed that writing was more than a means of communication. They saw it as a divine gift from Thoth himself, enabling the preservation and dissemination of knowledge across generations.

Thoth's reputation as a god of wisdom and knowledge was not confined to the borders of Egypt. His influence reached the shores of Greece, where he was revered as Hermes Trismegistus. This syncretic figure, a blend of the Egyptian Thoth and the Greek Hermes, shows the existence of cross-cultural exchange between these two great civilizations. Hermes Trismegistus embodied the qualities of both gods, and he was revered as a messenger and a mediator.

In Greece, Thoth-Hermes Trismegistus was celebrated as the god of wisdom and the patron of esoteric knowledge. He influenced religious thought, alchemy, and the early foundations of science. The Greeks saw in Hermes Trismegistus a deity who transcended the physical world, offering a bridge to the divine and unlocking the secrets of the universe.

Thoth's role as the god of wisdom and the creator of knowledge was thus a cornerstone in the intellectual and spiritual heritage of Egypt and the wider ancient world. His teachings, whether in the form of religious texts, philosophical treatises, or scientific observations, were considered to be divine revelations, offering guidance and enlightenment to those who sought to understand the deeper truths of existence. In every stroke of a scribe's pen, in every incantation uttered by a magician, and in every decision made by a judge, the presence of Thoth was felt.

Thoth's wisdom and cunning not only earned him a revered place among the mortals but also made him a pivotal figure in the tales of gods. His involvement in the divine dramas of the Egyptian pantheon showcased his ingenuity and resourcefulness, making him an indispensable ally to the other gods. One such tale involves Ra and a particular deity—some claim her to be the sun god's daughter—known as the Distant Goddess.

In this legend, the Distant Goddess was said to be Hathor, also known as the Eye of Ra. She was the goddess of many things, including love, beauty, music, dancing, fertility, and pleasure. The story began when the goddess, in a fit of anger, momentarily broke away from the established order. Perhaps disenchanted and seeking solitude, she transformed into a fierce feline, a move that represented freedom and untamed nature. She fled into the desert, leaving behind her responsibilities and her father, Ra, the sun god. In her absence, a sense of imbalance pervaded, as if the earth itself yearned for her return.

Ra was deeply concerned by her absence and its effects on the land, so he turned to Thoth for assistance. Thoth, who was known for his wisdom and persuasive abilities, was tasked with the crucial mission of bringing her back.

The journey to retrieve the Distant Goddess was not one of brute force or coercion. Instead, Thoth used his skills of diplomacy and understanding. While disguised as either a baboon or a monkey, Thoth approached her. He recognized her grievances and acknowledged her autonomy. Through clever dialogue and patient negotiation, he persuaded her to return. One source claims the god had to persuade her 1,077 times before she agreed.

The return of the Distant Goddess brought rejuvenation to the world. Her return heralded the inundation of the Nile, an event that brought life-giving waters to the people of Egypt. However, the goddess's return was contingent on more than just the desire of Ra or the needs of the people. She had to be appeased and honored with jubilant festivities. Music, dancing, feasting, and drunken revelry were essential rituals to placate the goddess and ensure her benevolence.

# Chapter 7: Horus the Falcon King

Isis was alone now that Osiris had departed to the land of the dead to preside over the souls of the deceased. Knowing that Set would do everything in his power to remain on the throne of Egypt, the goddess made haste to retreat into the shadows of the Nile Delta. She knew she had to protect her son, Horus, especially since Osiris himself had prophesied that their son would bring honor back to the family name. After enduring hours of extreme labor, Isis gave birth to Horus. She began raising him the best she could, putting his safety above all.

To avoid danger, the goddess chose to only emerge out of the secluded marshland at night. This was when she would go and search for food to keep herself and her only son alive. However, Isis was not alone. She was protected by a bodyguard of seven scorpions, which belonged to the goddess of healing and poison, Serket (who we will discuss further later on). However, Isis still had to be on alert at all times since Set had installed eyes nearly everywhere. While Isis was out looking for food, Horus would be left with Serket, who nurtured him. Horus eventually grew into a god of formidable stature.

Horus showed signs of divinity and extraordinary power the very moment he arrived in the world. One of his eyes was said to have glowed as bright as the sun, while the other appeared as luminous as the moon. He also had the head of a falcon, which represented the keen vision and soaring spirit of the bird. His physical prowess was impressive and was matched by his sharp intellect. The ancient Egyptians believed that his gaze could pierce through untruths. Later on, the people would depict the god wearing the double crown of Egypt, signifying his dominion over both the physical world and the celestial realm.

The son of Osiris and Isis also displayed a keen sense of awareness and unyielding spirit from an early age. As he grew up, Isis began instilling in him the virtues of justice, honor, and compassion. The goddess also taught him the secrets of the gods and filled his childhood with stories of the land. She worked hard to prepare him for the day when he claimed his throne. Of course, her teachings were not of vengeance or hatred; Isis taught him to understand the delicate balance that governs all existence.

Eventually, Horus developed traits that endeared him to all of creation. He was brave, not in the sense of a warrior but as one who faces the unknown with unwavering resolve. His wisdom was evident in his thoughtful demeanor. He always considered the consequences of his actions on the cosmic balance. And above all, he was just, a quality he held most dear since it reflected his inherent role as a future upholder of Ma'at, the ancient Egyptian concept of truth and order.

Meanwhile, the land of Egypt was plunged into turmoil under the rule of Set. The once flourishing kingdom, which had been nourished by the wise rule of Osiris and the nurturing care of Isis, withered under the grip of chaos and disorder.

Horus, the falcon-headed god.[17]

Under Osiris, Egypt had been a land of plenty. The god-king, together with Isis, had introduced the art of agriculture and culture to humanity. Their reign was a golden era, marked by bountiful harvests and rivers teeming with fish. The fields of Egypt were lush with grain, and the granaries overflowed with the rewards of a well-tended earth. The people thrived. Their needs were fulfilled, and their lives were enriched by the blessings of their divine rulers.

But with Set upon the throne, the prosperous land transformed for the worse. Where there was once abundance, there was famine in the cities and villages. The Nile, which had faithfully nourished the land, flooded unpredictably or withheld its life-giving waters, leaving the fields parched and barren. Crops withered, and hunger crept into homes that had once known only plenty.

The skies mirrored the chaos below. Once clear and bright, they were often shrouded in ominous clouds, casting shadows over the land. Plagues sickened both livestock and people, adding to the growing despair.

Social order, which had been the centerpiece of Egyptian life under Osiris and Isis, greatly declined under Set's rule. Where there had been justice and fairness, now there was only the whim of a tyrant. Previously, the people looked toward the throne for guidance and protection, but with Set on top, they could only feel the heavy yoke of oppression. It became increasingly clear that the throne belonged to someone of pure heart—someone who could mirror the previous king. Perhaps a direct descendant of the great Osiris himself.

When Horus finally reached adulthood, he knew it was time to gather his strength, reclaim his birthright, and restore Egypt to its former glory. Horus was said to have first approached the gods to stake his claim. Standing before a court of the Great Ennead, which included Set himself and was presided by Ra, he laid forth his case. He pointed his finger at Set, claiming that he had unlawfully usurped the throne. He exclaimed that Egypt had been in turmoil under the god of chaos for too long and that it was time for Set to step down.

The gods listened intently as Horus made his plea. They saw in him the potential for a great king, one who could blend Osiris's just rule with his own unique strengths. Many viewed Horus as the beacon of hope that Egypt desperately needed.

Ra was not as easily swayed by his speech. While some suggested he had an issue with Horus's young age and inexperience, others whispered that the sun god actually harbored sympathy for Set. The god of chaos might have unleashed havoc across the kingdom, but he was a loyal companion in Ra's nightly battles against Apophis. The divine assembly failed to reach a consensus. Opinions were clearly divided.

Knowing that Horus would not leave empty-handed, Ra came up with a pronouncement. The decision of who would ascend to the throne of Egypt would not be made by divine decree alone. Instead, it would be determined through a series of contests between Horus and Set. The winner of these trials would prove their worthiness to rule and would be crowned as the rightful king.

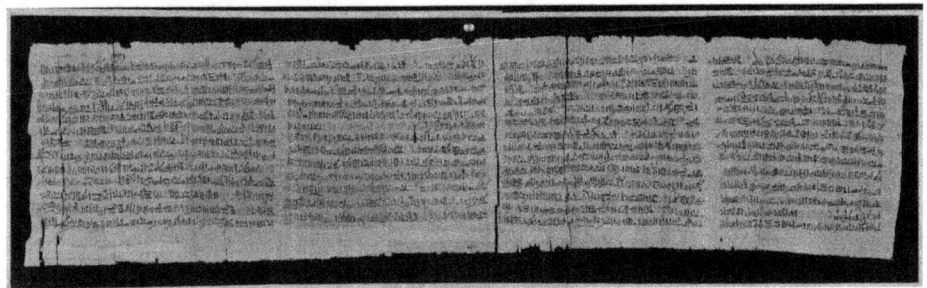

The manuscript detailing the events of "The Contendings of Horus and Set."[38]

The first trial was rather peculiar. It was chosen by none other than the god of chaos himself. The test was to see who among the two contending gods could remain underwater the longest. Both Set and Horus had to transform themselves into hippopotami before submerging themselves into the Nile. Whoever succeeded in remaining underwater for three consecutive months would be declared the winner.

When the day of the trial arrived, the banks of the Nile were alive with anticipation. Not only had the mighty gods and goddesses gathered to watch the trial, but the banks were also filled with spirits and creatures of all kinds. Set, ever confident, morphed first. His hippo form was massive, complete with thick skin and powerful jaws. When he snapped his jaws shut, a loud sound pierced the air, frightening even the mightiest of animals present. Then, Horus transformed, taking on the hefty and robust form of a hippopotamus. He did not display any act of boastful bravery like his uncle. Instead, he remained calm as he surveyed his surroundings.

After being given the green light to begin the trial, Horus and Set plunged into the Nile. Silence replaced the anticipation in the air as the two gods disappeared beneath the surface. The first few days passed slowly, yet neither god was planning on coming to the surface anytime soon. They both maintained their positions underwater, putting their endurance to the ultimate test. When days turned into weeks, the interest and anxiety among the gods grew.

Isis watched the test with growing concern. She was beginning to feel torn between her maternal instincts and the rules of the contest. Eventually, the goddess chose to intervene. Using her magic, she crafted a copper harpoon. She then stealthily approached the Nile and hurled the harpoon into the depths, hoping to hit Set and disturb his focus.

Unfortunately, her aim was miscalculated. Instead of piercing Set, the harpoon struck her own son. However, Isis was quick enough to correct her mistake. Again, she prepared another harpoon and hurled it directly at Set. This time around, the harpoon found its mark, wounding Set. Perhaps startled and in pain, the god of chaos rose to the surface, surprising many.

In a turn of events, Set went to Isis. He did not approach the goddess in a rage. Instead, he played on their familial ties and asked her to heal his wounds. Although she was loyal to Horus, Isis eventually relented after finding herself swayed by her brother's pleas. The goddess healed Set's injuries. Of course, this did not go unnoticed. Horus emerged from the Nile, ready to express his fury following his mother's actions. Feeling betrayed, Horus impulsively decapitated Isis, shocking the entire crowd of gods on the banks of the river.

Thankfully, Thoth was present during the episode. Ever the mediator and preserver of order, he intervened. Thoth made use of his precious knowledge of magic and healing to save Isis. According to some accounts, Thoth replaced Isis's severed head with that of a cow, which symbolized her nurturing and maternal attributes, thus preserving her life and divinity.

As for Horus, he retreated to a mountain. The angry god was hoping he could find solace after going through the test and being betrayed by his mother. Little did he know, but Set had been following his every movement. Taking opportunity of Horus's vulnerable state—he was beyond exhausted at that time—Set gouged out Horus's left eye.

Interestingly, this act not only intensified their rivalry; it also symbolized yet another natural occurrence. The left eye of Horus came to represent the waxing and waning phases of the moon. When his eye was taken away and damaged, it was associated with the new moon when the moon was not visible. The waxing moon, as it gained visibility, represented the eye being gradually restored, and the full moon signified the complete restoration of his eyes.

Horus, now injured and weakened, was tended to by Hathor. The goddess of love and beauty, known for her healing abilities, took Horus under her care. She nursed him back to health, tending to his wounds and aiding in the restoration of his lost eye.

The rivalry between the two contenders did not stop there. After recovering, Horus made sure to make a move; he was not planning on letting Set get away forever. This next episode came to be known as the infamous lettuce scene. According to tradition, Set had come up with a certain scheme. He hoped to discredit Horus by asserting his dominance sexually. The story goes that Set snuck into Horus's tent to sexually abuse him. Horus, however, had already devised a strategy to thwart his uncle's devious plan. He quietly caught Set's seed in his hand. Horus did not confront Set immediately but instead sought the counsel of his mother, Isis.

The goddess devised a plan to turn the situation to Horus's advantage. She advised Horus to dispose of Set's seed in a way that would prevent it from being used against him. Following her guidance, Horus cast the seed into the river, ensuring that it would not serve as evidence of Set's dominance.

Of course, the plan did not end there. Isis then helped Horus craft his own seed and secretly placed it on Set's favorite food, which was lettuce. The plan worked without a hitch, and Set consumed the lettuce containing Horus's seed. When the time came for the gods to convene and judge the rightful ruler of Egypt, Set confidently proclaimed to the court that he had performed an act of dominance over Horus. Their stunned silence was broken when Horus stepped forward to deny the claim. He told the other gods that he was the one who had performed the act of dominance over Set. The gods did not know whose words were true, so they turned to Thoth to uncover the truth.

Thoth, using his divine abilities, called forth the seed of Set, expecting it to respond from within Horus. However, much to Set's surprise and embarrassment, it answered from the river, revealing his failure to dominate Horus. Thoth then called upon the seed of Horus. To the shock of many, the seed responded from within Set. This revelation turned the tables. Set, who had sought to humiliate Horus, found himself disgraced. The assembled gods laughed at Set's misfortune, and his claim to the throne was greatly weakened.

Still, their rivalry persisted for at least eighty years. The entire time, Ra continued to withhold his support from Horus, denying the son of Osiris his rightful claim to the throne. As a result, Egypt continued to spiral, as it suffered from mismanagement and neglect caused by Set. Isis could not bear to see the rivalry continue between the two. The stalemate had to end one way or the other, and Horus must sit on the throne. So, she transformed herself into a beautiful woman and made her way to Set's palace. Here, she began weeping, hoping to catch Set's attention.

Just as she suspected, the god of chaos was immediately drawn to the sight of this beautiful woman. Set asked her about the cause of her tears, to which Isis quickly spun a tale of woe. She told him of a cruel yet powerful man who had wronged her and her young son. She spoke of a story where the man denied them their rightful inheritance. Her story, though a fabrication, was laced with poignant details and delivered with such conviction that it stirred Set's emotions.

Set declared that such injustice was intolerable. He proclaimed that the man responsible for the young woman's suffering deserved severe punishment. He was so angry that he even swore a solemn oath to seek out this unjust man and cast him out of the lands. This was the moment Isis had been waiting for. She revealed her true identity, and unbeknownst to Set, they were not alone. Isis had gathered the other gods to witness Set's proclamations. Just like that, Set had unwittingly condemned himself. His promise to punish the man who caused the young woman's sorrow was, in fact, a self-indictment, as he was the one who had usurped the throne and caused suffering to Horus and Isis.

The irony of the situation was not lost on the assembled deities. Set, known for his cunning and trickery, had been outwitted by Isis's scheme. Ra, who had for so long resisted acknowledging Horus as the rightful king, could no longer deny the justice of his claim. The other gods, who had been divided in their support, now rallied behind Horus. Isis's intervention had not only exposed Set's hypocrisy but had also highlighted the righteousness of Horus's cause.

With Horus now on the throne, Egypt experienced an era of prosperity. Gone were the days of constant hunger, turmoil, and suffering. Horus's ascension to the throne was a moment of triumph, not just for him but for the ideals he represented: justice, rightful rule, and the restoration of order.

As for Set, he had to face the consequences of his actions. He was eventually banished to the dry and barren desert beyond the borders of Egypt. There is another tale that narrates his fate. According to this version of the myth, Set was presented before Horus in chains. To the surprise of many, Horus did not choose revenge. He understood the importance of cosmic balance and released Set instead of punishing him.

Horus acknowledged that chaos, as represented by Set, was an essential part of the natural order. He held to the belief that the world needed both stability and upheaval to maintain harmony. Set willingly retreated to the desert instead of being banished.

Horus's reign was one of spiritual and cultural rejuvenation. As a deity closely associated with the sky, the sun, and kingship, Horus became a symbol of power, vigor, and legitimacy. This connection between Horus and the monarchy was deeply ingrained in the Egyptian concept of divine kingship. The pharaohs of Egypt, regarded as living gods themselves, identified strongly with Horus. They were seen as earthly embodiments of the falcon-headed god, reigning with his authority, might, and divine right. This identification lent a sacred dimension to their rule, reinforcing their status as intermediaries between the gods and the people.

Upon their death, the pharaohs were then associated with Osiris, the god of the afterlife and resurrection. This transformation from being Horus in life to Osiris in death was integral to the Egyptian belief in the afterlife and the cyclical nature of kingship and divinity. This belief system reinforced the pharaoh's divine status and the perpetuity of his rule, even in the afterlife.

Temples dedicated to Horus rose majestically along the Nile. They served as places of worship and as centers of learning and administration. The cult of Horus played a significant role in the religious life of the Egyptians, influencing rituals, festivals, and the arts.

# Chapter 8: Serpent Magic and Transformation: Wadjet and Sobek

Many centuries before Egypt rose as the unified and powerful civilization that we remember today, the kingdom was a divided nation split into two distinct regions: Upper and Lower Egypt. Each region had its own unique cultural and political identity. Even the crown worn by their rulers (the term pharaoh was first used for Egyptian kings in the New Kingdom) were not the same. Those who had power in Lower Egypt (northern Egypt) wore the red crown known as the Deshret, while rulers of Upper Egypt (southern Egypt) adorned the tall white crown known as the Hedjet. Of course, these crowns were not just regal ornaments. They were also worn as powerful symbols of

The Hedjet crown of Upper Egypt (left) and the Deshret crown of Lower Egypt (right).²⁹

the ruler's authority and their connection to the gods.

The unification of Upper and Lower Egypt happened sometime around 3150 BCE. This unity brought about major changes across the land. It brought political and territorial cohesion, as well as a blending of cultural and religious symbols. One of the most prominent of these symbols was the Pschent. Often known simply as the double crown, it combined both elements of the Deshret and Hedjet. The Pschent, with its distinctive red and white elements, symbolized the ruler's dominion over both regions.

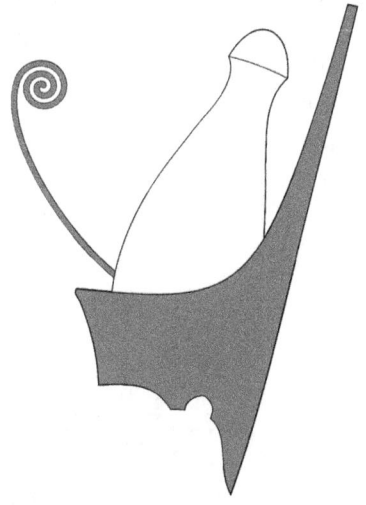

The double crown of unified Egypt.[80]

Tutankhamun's mask featuring a Uraeus.[81]

Central to the imagery of the pharaohs and their divine authority was the Uraeus, a stylized representation of a rearing cobra. Often affixed to the ruling pharaoh's headdress, the Uraeus symbolized royal authority, divine protection, and the fearsome power of the monarch. The rearing cobra was also a representation of the pharaoh's ability to ward off enemies who threatened his kingdom and evil spirits.

But why exactly did the Egyptians choose the cobra as the Uraeus? The significance of the Uraeus was, in fact, closely linked to a goddess known as Wadjet, which has been identified as one of the oldest deities in the Egyptian pantheon.

Wadjet, whose name meant "the green one," was a goddess whose influence and worship spanned the history of ancient Egyptian religion and culture. Initially a local goddess of the city Per-Wadjet (known to the Greeks as Buto), an important site in prehistoric Egypt, Wadjet's presence and significance evolved dramatically over the centuries. In her earliest representations during the predynastic period, Wadjet was depicted as a cobra, sometimes entwined around a papyrus stem, which perhaps symbolized her protective and nurturing nature.

**A representation of Wadjet as a snake.**[33]

As time progressed, depictions of Wadjet underwent a fascinating transformation. She was often portrayed as a woman with the head of a snake. Scholars suggest that this was a reflection of her dual nature as being both nurturing and fierce. At times, the Wadjet appeared as a lion-headed goddess, complete with the Uraeus on her head. This alternative image possibly signified royal power and authority. While her primary sacred animal was the cobra, the Late Period brought about an intriguing addition: the ichneumon. The ichneumon, a mongoose-like creature revered for its ability to kill snakes and crush crocodile eggs, became a sacred animal of Wadjet during this period.

The integration of the ichneumon into the worship of Wadjet was part of a broader pattern of religious syncretism prevalent during the Late Period. The deities of the Delta cities of Khem (Letopolis) and Per-Wadjet exemplified this trend. In these centers, the ichneumon, originally a sacred animal of Horus of Khem, was incorporated into the veneration of Wadjet of Per-Wadjet.

The reverence for the ichneumon in relation to Wadjet was distinct from that of other sacred animals. In artistic and religious representations, ichneumons were occasionally included in statuettes of Wadjet, particularly in her lion-headed form. These statuettes depicted the goddess seated on a throne, usually crowned by the Uraeus.

These statuettes often had a practical and spiritual function. The throne or the base attached to it, which was typically hollow, contained a mummified ichneumon. This practice reflected the ancient Egyptians' belief in the sacredness of animals and their role in the religious and spiritual realms.

The origins of the worship of Wadjet lay in Lower Egypt, where she was revered as the personification of the region. In fact, her temple in Per-Wadjet was not just a center of worship but also housed an oracle, believed by some to be a precursor to the oracle tradition in ancient Greece. This oracle was often consulted by pharaohs and commoners alike.

Depictions of Wadjet can be seen on the walls of various temples across Egypt. One notable example is in the Tomb of Nefertari, the wife of Ramesses II, where Wadjet is depicted as a winged cobra hovering protectively above Anubis. Her presence in such important burial sites underscored her role as a guardian deity. Additionally, Wadjet had a temple at the ancient site of Imet (now Tell Nebesha) in the Nile Delta, where she was worshiped as

Wadjet depicted in the Tomb of Nefertari above Anubis.[33]

the Lady of Imet. Over time, she formed part of a triad with Min (another one of the oldest Egyptian gods associated with fertility and harvest) and Horus.

Wadjet's counterpart was Nekhbet, another ancient deity who was often depicted alongside her. Nekhbet was represented as a vulture and was primarily associated with Upper Egypt, in contrast to Wadjet's affiliation with Lower Egypt. Together, Wadjet and Nekhbet were known as the "Two Ladies," a title embodying the unification of Upper and Lower Egypt. This epithet, Nebty, was frequently used in a pharaoh's title, symbolizing the pharaoh's sovereignty over both regions.

**Nekhbet as depicted in the tomb of Ramesses III.**[54]

The roles of the Two Ladies extended beyond the symbolism of unified Egypt. According to some versions, Wadjet and Nekhbet were also seen as key figures during the time when Isis was protecting her son Horus. According to legend, Wadjet was responsible for transforming parts of the Nile Delta into lush, papyrus-filled wetlands. She caused the papyrus plant to grow thick and tall, acting as a natural barrier. This was done to protect Isis and Horus from the prying eyes of Set.

Of course, apart from acting as protection for the divine mother and son, the papyrus plant served as one of Egypt's most precious resources. It was also highly sought after by not just the Egyptians but also those who came from beyond the continent. The plant was used to make paper, which was important for recording history, culture, and governmental administrative duties. The papyrus swamps also played a critical ecological role, supporting a diverse range of wildlife and serving as a natural barrier against invaders.

Nekhbet and Wadjet played a hand in nurturing the young Horus, especially when Isis was not around. They nurtured the young god physically and spiritually. Together, Nekhbet and Wadjet imparted strength and wisdom to Horus, both of which he would later use against Set and during his reign on the throne of Egypt.

## Sobek, the Crocodile God

It was common for the ancient Egyptians to see the divine in the most formidable of creatures. Take the Nile crocodiles. These fearsome beasts inhabited the river's murky depths and were held in high regard by the Egyptian civilization rather than despised for their vicious nature. To them, these crocodiles were considered sacred. It was of the utmost importance to please them if they wished not to taste their wrath. To appease these beasts, the Egyptians prayed to a certain deity, hoping they could calm the crocodiles and safeguard themselves from harm.

This particular deity was known as Sobek. Many view Sobek as the Egyptian god of protection. The truth, however, is rather more complex. While the crocodile god was considered a benevolent creature, he could also be unpredictable. While he was known to have the ability to ward off evil and protect the innocent, there were instances when Sobek displayed his aggressiveness and violence. Perhaps this was the very reason why he was also associated with military prowess.

Sobek had two different appearances. Most of the time, the god would appear as a muscular man with the head of a crocodile. To symbolize his divinity and power, Sobek wore an elaborate ceremonial headdress. Known as the Hemhem crown, it was said to have been a gift to the crocodile god by Ra. It was given as a reward for his military feats. Typically, the crown was often depicted with a ram's horns, a sun disk, and the Uraeus (the symbol of a rearing cobra, signifying divine authority). Sobek could also be depicted entirely as a crocodile. This version of the god was usually seen in temple reliefs that narrated stories of his role as the protector of the Nile.

At times, the crocodile god could be seen holding the ankh, which the Egyptians saw as a symbol of fertility. His Was scepter also denoted his royal god status, while the solar disk above his head linked him to the sun.

A relief from the Temple of Kom Ombo featuring Sobek in his crocodile-headed form.[85]

Although the god was known for his unpredictable nature, it is not fair to dismiss how important he was to the Nile. Certain ancient sources suggest that Sobek was the very god who created the Nile River. The river was believed to have originated from his own sweat. Because of his status as the god of fertility, the water lily could also appear in his depictions, symbolizing regeneration and rebirth.

Sobek's worship was especially prominent in areas where crocodiles called home. His worship was mainly focused in Shedet, later known as Crocodilopolis. This major cult center, situated in the lush Faiyum region, became the heart of the worship of Sobek, especially during the Middle Kingdom when his significance in the Egyptian pantheon notably increased.

The temples dedicated to Sobek in Crocodilopolis were unique, as they often housed live crocodiles that were raised for religious purposes. These crocodiles were considered to be living incarnations of Sobek himself. Because of that, they were treated with great reverence and care since they were thought to be sacred beings. The death of a crocodile was not taken lightly. More often than not, the ancient Egyptians performed rituals for these sacred crocodiles. These rituals were usually done at the main temple in Crocodilopolis, with the crocodiles being treated as the earthly manifestations of Sobek.

The remains of crocodiles were treated with absolute care as well. They were mummified and stored safely. Interestingly, some of these mummified crocodiles have been found with baby crocodiles in their mouths or on their backs. This aspect of the crocodile's behavior, diligent in caring for its young, was preserved through mummification, symbolizing the protective and nurturing nature of Sobek.

The mummified crocodiles were not only kept in temples. They were also sometimes buried with pharaohs or nobles. It was believed that these sacred animals would continue to provide protection in the afterlife, guarding the deceased against any harm.

Mummified crocodiles at the Temple of Kom Ombo.[86]

In addition to Crocodilopolis, another key location in the worship of Sobek was Kom Ombo. This site was initially shared by Sobek and Horus as patrons. However, a myth recounts that a disagreement between the two deities led to Sobek expelling Horus from the temple. This act brought misfortune to the area, manifesting as a plague. Realizing the gravity of his actions, Sobek called upon Horus to return, restoring their joint patronage over Kom Ombo. The temple became a dual sanctuary, honoring both Sobek and Horus.

Aside from Crocodilopolis, Sobek was also worshiped by people in Kom Ombo. Initially, the site was under the protection of two gods: Sobek and Horus. However, legend has it that the two deities once became embroiled in a heated disagreement. This resulted in Sobek expelling Horus from Kom Ombo. Unfortunately, Sobek's impulsive action brought misfortune to the area. A plague razed the population, killing even the strongest humans. After finally realizing that the plague was the consequence of his actions, Sobek recalled Horus, restoring their joint patronage over Kom Ombo. From then on, the temple at Kom Ombo continued as a dual sanctuary. Those who visited were allowed to pay their respects to both Horus and Sobek.

Similar to Osiris, Anubis, and other prominent gods of the Egyptian pantheon, Sobek went through a period of transformation over time. The ancient Egyptians began associating Sobek more with the sun god Ra. They eventually merged these two divine figures, creating Sobek-Ra. This elevated Sobek's status further. Besides being honored for creating and protecting the Nile, Sobek was also linked to the great power of the sun.

Sobek's influence could be felt in various aspects of Egyptian culture, particularly in royal ideology. One of the most striking examples is the story of Sobekneferu, the first recorded female pharaoh of the kingdom. Having ruled at the close of the Twelfth Dynasty, her name means the "Beauty of Sobek." The pharaoh's decision to include Sobek in her name showed the high esteem in which the crocodile deity was held during her time. Not only did this indicate her ultimate devotion to Sobek, but Sobekneferu was also seeking divine endorsement to reinforce her authority in both the political and religious realms. Although her reign was relatively brief, it marked a period in which the cult of Sobek (especially the version where he was merged with Ra) gained more prominence within state worship and royal identity.

While the inclusion of Sobek's name in her title can be interpreted as a reflection of her desire to align her rule with the attributes associated with Sobek—strength, protection, and rejuvenation—some sources also suspected that this action served a critical political purpose. Although Egyptian women had more rights compared to other ancient cultures like the Greeks or the Romans, to rule a kingdom as a female pharaoh was still a challenge. Female pharaohs often found themselves facing the challenging task of asserting their authority in a predominantly male-dominated sphere. Therefore, this strategic use of Sobek's name can be interpreted as Sobekneferu's way of infusing her rule with a sense of masculinity and divine power, characteristics traditionally associated with male pharaohs. It was a means to solidify her position and proclaim her power in a society where female pharaohs were rarities.

Of course, Sobekneferu was not the only female leader known to have assumed aspects of male divinity to assert her rule. The same could be said about Hatshepsut, who ruled much later. Hoping to assert her authority in a patriarchal society, Hatshepsut famously donned the regalia and symbols of a male ruler in official ceremonies. Even her statues were often depicted with a false beard and a nemes headdress, the striped headcloth typically worn by male kings of Egypt. However, despite Hatshepsut's many contributions to the kingdom, the pharaoh failed to escape the act of *damnatio memoriae*, the condemnation of memory. Her inscriptions and monuments were later destroyed by her rivals who wished to erase her from history; this clearly failed since her name is known to us today.

Despite the challenges faced by Sobekneferu and Hatshepsut in asserting their authority in a patriarchal society, it is important to note that Egypt had several other female rulers who successfully navigated the complexities of leadership in ancient times. These women demonstrated remarkable resilience and adaptability, often utilizing similar strategies to assert their rule and leave their mark on Egyptian history.

Sobek's evolution from a feared deity of the Nile to a figure embodying both protection and royal authority, especially in his merged form with Ra, underscores the Egyptians' deep connection to and reverence for the natural world and its deities. His influence, evident in the reigns of pharaohs like Sobekneferu, highlights the role of gods in legitimizing and guiding rulership.

# Chapter 9: Lesser-Known Deities: A Case Study

While the likes of Osiris, Isis, and Ra often dominate the narrative with their prominent roles and well-known legends, there is a group of lesser-known but equally intriguing gods and goddesses who wielded a lot of influence in various aspects of ancient Egyptian culture. This particular chapter is reserved for these deities. We will talk about Seshat, the goddess of writing; Khnum, the divine potter; Serket, the scorpion goddess of healing and protection; and Babi, the fierce baboon god of the underworld.

## Seshat, the Goddess of Many Responsibilities

Seshat played an important role in the daily and ceremonial life of this ancient civilization. Her name, translating to "female scribe," hints at her primary role in Egyptian society.

Seshat often appeared as a woman wearing a leopard skin draped over her robe. Her headdress was rather unique. She did not wear an elaborate crown full of precious stones and gems but

A carving of Seshat at the Temple of Luxor, dating from 1250 BCE.⁸⁷

rather a simple seven-pointed star arched by a crescent bow. Unfortunately, not much evidence survived that could explain the meaning behind her appearance. Some scholars suggest that her crown represented her connection to the heavens or perhaps was a symbol of precision and dexterity. Others claim it indicated her celestial stature. Her leopard skin was linked to power and control over danger. Leopards were seen as fierce predators.

Even her origins are shrouded in mystery. Some claimed she was related to the god of wisdom and writing, Thoth—she was either his wife or daughter. This connection is further emphasized by the differing views regarding the development of the writing system in ancient Egypt. While some sources attribute this monumental advancement to Thoth, others believe it was Seshat who created it. Only then did Thoth teach it to humanity. According to Egyptologist Richard H. Wilkinson, Seshat frequently appeared in reliefs and inscriptions, especially those dating from the Early Dynastic Period, as the goddess of measurements and writing, which clearly indicated her significance from very early on.

Seshat was also considered the patroness of libraries and librarians. She was said to have played a major role in the maintenance and preservation of knowledge. Her responsibilities included record-keeping, accounting, measurements, and census-taking. Of course, her role as a record-keeper was not limited to mundane affairs. During the Middle Kingdom era, she documented the spoils of war, including animals and captives, and kept track of tributes related to the king. During the New Kingdom, her association with the pharaoh became more pronounced, as she was believed to have recorded the years of his reign and the jubilee festivals, particularly the Sed festival, a ceremony that celebrated the continued rule and rejuvenation of the pharaoh.

Seshat was credited as the keeper of the House of Life, which was an institution that functioned as a library, university, and research center. This was where one could find an array of spiritual and practical knowledge in both written and pictorial forms. Of course, the goddess's influence was not only limited to writing and record-keeping. Seshat was also revered in the realm of architecture and construction; she was thought to be the patroness of builders. Legend has it that Seshat played a role in assisting pharaohs in the "stretching the cord" ritual, a foundational ceremony for temple-building that involved laying out the architectural plan.

In the realm of the dead, Seshat was seen as a friend of the deceased. At times, her image appeared alongside Nephthys in scenes of restoring the limbs of the departed.

Interestingly, despite her many responsibilities and the significance of her role, Seshat never had her own temples, cults, or formal worship. However, the high value placed on writing and construction in Egyptian society meant that she was venerated widely through everyday acts and daily rituals. From the Early Dynastic Period to the rule of the Ptolemaic dynasty, her presence was a constant in the lives of the ancient Egyptians. In this way, Seshat's influence, though less conspicuous than that of other deities, was deeply embedded in the culture and spirituality of ancient Egypt, leaving a lasting imprint on the civilization.

## Khnum, the Ram-Headed God Who Shaped Mankind

Khnum was yet another one of the Egyptian gods depicted with the head of an animal; he had the head of a ram. Primarily recognized as the guardian of the source of the Nile, Khnum carried a responsibility that linked him to the life-giving properties of the river. In ancient Egypt, a ram was seen as a symbol of fertility and strength. Therefore, his depiction was fitting for a god believed to have control over the Nile's inundation. Khnum's guardianship over this process was critical to the survival and prosperity of ancient Egyptians, making him a deity of immense importance, particularly to those whose lives were closely tied to the river and its cycles.

Khnum's worship centers were primarily located at the First Cataract of the Nile, particularly on the island of

A depiction of the ram-headed god, Khnum.[38]

Elephantine. Here, at the supposed source of the Nile, one could find a few of his temples and shrines. They were typically constructed and cared for by those whose lives were inextricably linked to the river. Without Khnum, their lives would not be prosperous, so it was important to hold the god in high regard.

Interestingly, Khnum was revered by the ancient Egyptians as the god of creation. According to tradition, he was believed to have been the divine potter who molded humans on his potter's wheel. After shaping a person from clay, Khnum breathed life into it, giving them a ka or a spirit. This scene of creation often made an appearance in temple reliefs and art. Typically, Khnum would be depicted by his potter's wheel as he carefully shaped an individual. Other ancient sources credited the ram-headed god with the creation of the "first egg of the world." This narrative placed him at the very heart of the universe's genesis, as this particular divine egg was believed to be the source of all creation, including life, the sun, and the cosmos.

A relief of Khnum creating a human being on his divine potter's wheel.[39]

The most enthralling story involving the ram-headed god is the one linked to Pharaoh Djoser and a great famine that struck the kingdom during his reign. This particular event was recorded clearly on the Famine Stela, which survived the test of time. According to this ancient source, Egypt once suffered a severe famine that plagued its people for seven years. Djoser, who was pharaoh at the time, spent day and night trying to save his people from the catastrophe. Seeing no other way, the pharaoh turned to divine intervention. He prayed to Khnum, hoping the god could assist in ending the drought.

Legend has it that the pharaoh had a dream afterward. In his sleep, he was met with the ram-headed deity, who promised the pharaoh to end the suffering should he agree to a condition. Khnum instructed Djoser to rebuild and fix the dilapidated temple of Khnum on Elephantine. After being awoken from his mysterious dream, Djoser did not waste any time doing exactly what the god had instructed him. He launched a reconstruction project to repair the temple, and just as Khnum had promised, Egypt was immediately healed. The annual flooding finally came to revitalize the crops, restoring the kingdom's agricultural abundance and saving the people from terrible hunger.

Djoser was not the only pharaoh whose story intertwined with Khnum. The female queen, Hatshepsut, was also said to have dealings with the ram-headed god. According to this story, Amun-Ra, disguised as Thutmose I (Hatshepsut's father), visited her mother. It was from this divine union that Hatshepsut was conceived. Khnum was thought to have been the one who breathed life into Hatshepsut, imbuing her with the essence of divinity and kingship. This narrative not only portrays Khnum's role as a giver of life, but it also ties him to the legitimization of royal power, something a female pharaoh needed since they had to navigate a patriarchal society to assert her authority.

Khnum's influence declined over time, overshadowed by other more prominent deities like Ra, Amun, and Osiris. However, the god's name was never completely erased in the story of ancient Egypt. His name was invoked by the Egyptians once in a while, and inscriptions of him survived for many centuries.

### Serket, the Protective Scorpion Goddess

Serket, whose name means "she who causes the throat to breathe," was a multifaceted goddess who many agree transcends the simple categorization often found in ancient mythologies. Though there are no mythological tales detailing the goddess's origin unlike many deities in Egyptian mythology, her influence and presence in ancient Egyptian culture and religion are indeed vast. She had been worshiped largely in Lower Egypt since the Predynastic Period.

The scorpion goddess, Serket as seen in the Tomb of Nefertari.⁴⁶

Although her origin and background remain a subject of debate among scholars, historians, and Egyptologists, Serket's depictions are rather rich and symbolic. More often than not, she appeared on the walls of temples and tombs as a female human with a scorpion sitting on her head. Other times, Serket was depicted as a scorpion with the head of a woman. Scholars suggest that this duality of human and scorpion form meant she was a goddess who mediated between the natural and supernatural worlds.

The most popular myth featuring Serket was the one involving Isis and her son, Horus. This particular myth offers a glimpse into her protective and vengeful sides. The story goes that Serket played a role in assisting Isis with protecting Horus from the wrath of the god of chaos, Set. It was believed that Isis herself was protected by seven of Serket's scorpions. Three scorpions named Petet, Tjetet, and Matet would scout ahead, ensuring Isis and Horus could pass safely. Two more, Masetet and Mesetetef, would remain by her side, while another two, Befen and Tefen (considered the fiercest of all seven scorpions), guarded the goddess from the rear in case Set ever planned an ambush from behind.

There was a time when Isis, in the disguise of a poor woman, journeyed to an unknown town. Here, she begged for some food and shelter for the night. However, Isis was not met with kindness. Instead, she had to face the scorn of a wealthy noblewoman who slammed the door on the disguised goddess, denying her hospitality. Serket was said to have witnessed the incident through the eyes of her scorpions. She was infuriated. Serket commanded her most loyal and fiercest scorpion, Tefen, to teach the noblewoman a lesson for her unkindness.

Tefen had the other scorpions surrender their poison to him, creating one that was strong enough to kill a human. He planned to inject the poison not into the noblewoman herself but her son.

As for Isis, she eventually found compassion from a poor peasant woman. Although she did not have much to offer, the woman gave the goddess a simple meal and offered her a bed to rest for the night. Delighted, Isis sat and ate with the woman that night. This was the moment Tefen had been waiting for. Knowing that Isis was safe for the moment, the scorpion was able to leave her side and exact revenge—or a lesson—on the noblewoman. Tefen stung the noblewoman's son, who, within seconds, dropped unconscious to the floor. Panicked, the noblewoman scrambled to help her son, attempting to revive him to no avail.

The noblewoman's despair eventually led her to Isis. The goddess, known for her compassion and motherly attributes, chose to heal the child despite the earlier rebuff. Legend has it that Isis invoked the secret names of the scorpions, neutralizing the poison with her powerful healing magic. This act of mercy not only revived the innocent child but also transformed the noblewoman's heart. Feeling ashamed of her earlier actions, she offered Isis her wealth as a token of gratitude.

Serket, who had been observing these events from the swampy marshland, felt remorse for her hasty decision to harm the innocent child. From then on, she vowed to protect all children.

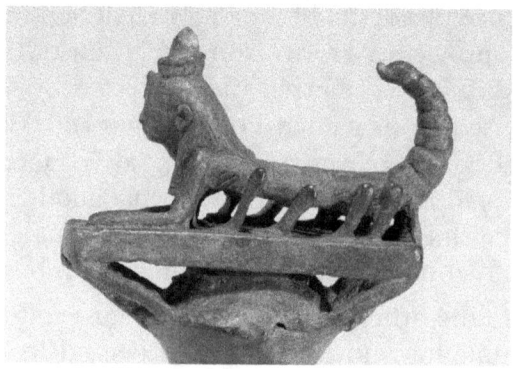

Serket as a scorpion.[41]

Serket also played a crucial role in the underworld. The scorpion goddess was tasked with overseeing the souls of the deceased. The Egyptians believed that Serket's magical abilities could help the dead breathe again as they were reborn from their bodies, hence the meaning behind her name. She was both a rewarder of the justified and a punisher of the unworthy. While some believed that the unworthy were condemned straight to oblivion when their heart was devoured by Ammit, others believed that instead of ceasing to exist, their souls would be forever tormented by Serket.

However, Serket's wrath was not confined only to the netherworld. On earth, she and her scorpions would often wander the vast lands, exacting retribution on those who preyed on the innocent or engaged in wickedness. Interestingly, the venom of her scorpions varied in intensity. Some scorpion stings could only cause pain, while others had the capability to cause breathlessness or, worse, bring about their death.

As a goddess associated with death, she played a role in safeguarding the internal organs of the dead, particularly the intestines, which were associated with poison. She protected Qebehsenuef, one of the four sons of Horus, who was in charge of the intestines in the canopic jars.

Despite being categorized as a lesser goddess, Serket held a revered position in Egyptian religion. True, she did not have grand temples built in her honor. Yet, Serket had loyal followers. Known as the Followers of Serket, they were typically made up of physicians and healers adept in both medical and spiritual practices. Her cult was open to both men and women. They were typically known for their proficiency in medicine and the rites of Serket, which involved invoking her for healing. Spells in her name were commonly used for driving out poisons and ensuring good health.

### Babi, the Bloodthirsty Baboon God

The ancient Egyptians considered the hamadryas baboon a sacred animal. Distinguishable by its grey streak of hair, this species of baboon was thought to have possessed the power to intercede with gods on behalf of humans. The Egyptians honored these primates with sacrifices and offerings. They believed that these acts could protect them from earthly evils and ensure a safe afterlife.

The belief that baboons were reincarnations of deceased loved ones further elevated their sacred status. Egyptians saw in baboons a reflection of their own society, making them ideal candidates for the embodiment of the human soul. This connection was deepened by the popular belief that baboons could communicate with Ra, the sun god. Their morning rituals of loud calls and stretching postures were interpreted as a form of worship or communication with Ra.

Babi, also known as Baba, simply means the "chief of baboons." Unlike the typical portrayal of gods as benevolent and virtuous, Babi is often depicted as having aggressive and lustful traits. This depiction draws from the nature of baboons, which are known for their aggression and high libido, influencing the perception of Babi as a bloodthirsty deity who lived on the entrails of the unworthy.

A common depiction of Babi, who is crouched with an erection.⁴⁸

In the afterlife, Babi's role was equally significant and daunting. He was believed to be the devourer of the souls of the unrighteous, similar to another creature known as Ammit (often depicted with the head of a crocodile, the front legs of a lion, and the hindquarters of a hippopotamus). While Ammit often appeared in many Egyptian texts, feared yet respected as the creature that devoured the heart of the unworthy, Babi appeared in other versions of the afterlife journey as an underworld ape god who fed on human entrails and unworthy souls.

His association with virility in the afterlife stems from the high libido observed in baboons. Many depictions of Babi show him with an erect penis, which was seen as a symbol of power and sexual prowess. In some beliefs, this attribute of Babi was thought to serve as a mast for the ferryboat that transported the unrighteous to the underworld, linking him to the journey of the soul after death.

Babi was worshiped most prominently in Hermopolis, known today as El Ashmunein. His worshipers sought his favor for a sexually active afterlife and protection from the horrors of hell. To avoid the wrath of Babi, Egyptians employed spells and magical rituals, particularly in the Hall of Two Truths, where the fate of the soul was determined after death.

The worship of Babi, however, witnessed a significant decline during the reign of Pharaoh Akhenaten, who introduced monotheism with a focus on the worship of the sun god, Amun-Ra. The worship of multiple deities was gradually replaced by the singular worship of Amun-Ra, though the worship of other deities, such as Osiris, Isis, and Horus, was eventually brought back with the rise of Tutankhamun, Akhenaten's son.

Babi's portrayal as a bloodthirsty, virile deity contrasts sharply with the conventional benevolent god figure, offering a glimpse into the Egyptians' great reverence and fear of the natural world. The worship of Babi highlights the intricate relationship between humans, animals, and gods in ancient Egyptian culture.

**The Mysterious Medjed**

Out of all of the lesser-known deities of the Egyptian pantheon, Medjed stands as one of the most obscure. Mentions of the god first appeared during the New Kingdom, yet his origins remain elusive. Medjed was also mentioned briefly in the Book of the Dead, specifically in the seventeenth chapter. This passage listed various divine beings who resided in the afterlife, so it is safe to assume that Medjed had an important role in the realm of the dead. However, while many other gods of Egypt were listed alongside their own stories and myths and had temples built in their honor, Medjed was the complete opposite. There was no temple or structure erected in dedication to the deity.

However, what truly captured the attention of modern-day people was not just his obscurity but also the way he was depicted and drawn. On a handful of papyri uncovered from the Late Period, Medjed was depicted as a floating figure with a rounded white body. It was as if he was cloaked in a sheet, like a ghost. On his face was only a pair of eyes, and Medjed also had two legs poking out from beneath. The deity had no arms or mouth, only a pair of eyes and feet that looked like sticks. This was indeed a stark contrast compared to the drawings and hieroglyphs of other deities in the pantheon. While figures like Serket, Khnum, and even Seshat were often depicted in a more serious manner, Medjed is seen by modern eyes as more cartoonish. Regardless of his depiction, Medjed might have had a bigger role in the mythical world of Egypt than is commonly thought.

The Book of the Dead, for instance, referred to Medjed as "the smiter." The reason behind this is uncertain. He was believed to have been able to shoot light from his eyes. Some interpret this as Medjed shooting deadly beams of light, similar to eye lasers. There is also a passage in the Book of the Dead that speaks about how Medjed could pass unseen among men. The exact meaning behind this remains a subject of debate. Some scholars suggest Medjed was a symbol of divine justice in its purest, most unpredictable form. His simple, shrouded appearance might reflect his invisibility to the human eye, with his true form hidden beneath a veil.

What we can be sure of is that Medjed was a crucial figure in the afterlife. He was thought to have been a protector of the dead. He was one of the many deities who assisted the souls of the departed with crossing through the various stages of the Du'at. He stood by them, offering guidance and safeguarding souls from any harm imposed by demons.

Medjed recently garnered attention from all over the world. It all began when the Greenfield Papyrus (a document dating from the Third Intermediate Period), which contained a depiction of the minor god, was put on display at the Mori Art Museum in Tokyo and, later, the Fukuoka Museum of Art. Here, a range of Egyptian gods was introduced to a wider audience, but Medjed caught the attention of many. This was largely due to his peculiar depiction. Medjed became an internet sensation in Japan. The Egyptian god was featured in video games and animated shows and even turned into plushies.

In many ways, Medjed's unexpected rise from obscurity to modern pop culture emphasizes the timeless appeal of Egypt's rich mythology. Although Medjed had once been a nearly forgotten figure whose name was mentioned only a handful of times, he now stands as a reminder that even the most mysterious figures can find new life across time and cultures.

# Chapter 10: The Impact of Egyptian Mythology on Modern Culture

It is safe to say that the stories and legends of Egypt are not confined only to the ancient past. The compelling narratives of these gods and goddesses, from the most popular ones such as Ra, Set, Isis, and Osiris to the less well-known deities such as Seshat and Babi, and the themes of creation, power, and the underworld have left a lasting imprint that extends far beyond their origins in the sands of Egypt. This final chapter aims to shift our focus from the historical and mythological realms to the contemporary world.

In contemporary literature, the allure of Egyptian mythology has not waned. Modern novels, often seen as gateways to fantasy and adventure, have embraced these ancient narratives, weaving them into stories that resonate with today's readers. A prime example is Rick Riordan's *The Kane Chronicles*, where the rich tapestry of Egyptian myths is brought to life through the eyes of modern characters. Riordan's work blends the ancient and the contemporary, introducing a younger generation to the likes of Osiris, Isis, and Set in a setting they can relate to. This blend of old and new not only entertains but also educates, creating a bridge between the past and the present.

Poetry and plays also find inspiration in Egyptian mythology. They often use mythological references and symbols to explore themes such as life, death, and rebirth. The ancient stories, with their deep philosophical undertones, offer a rich well from which poets and playwrights draw. Whether it's a poem that subtly alludes to the journey of Ra across the sky or a play that centers around the power struggles of the gods, these works bring a piece of ancient Egypt into contemporary literary culture.

The influence of these myths in modern literature is not just about retelling old stories. It is also about reinterpretation and relevance. Contemporary authors and playwrights reinvent these myths, often infusing them with modern themes and perspectives. This reimagining is crucial since it keeps the myths alive, dynamic, and pertinent to current societal contexts.

Of course, the reimagining of Egyptian myths also extends into the visually striking world of film and television. However, compared to the wealth of content inspired by Greek mythology, the foray into Egyptian myths in film and television is relatively less trodden. This scarcity makes the existing works particularly important in keeping the legacy of Egyptian mythology visible in popular culture. Each film or series, by virtue of its rarity, becomes a precious window into the world of ancient Egyptian gods, legends, and lore, invoking curiosity and fascination among audiences.

Blockbuster movies like *The Mummy* series, for example, have played a great role in bringing these ancient tales to a global audience. These films, with their blend of action, adventure, a pinch of comedy, and colorful mythological elements, offer a cinematic interpretation of Egypt's rich mythological history. The portrayal of mummies, curses, and other prominent historical figures in these movies, while often dramatized, has introduced Egyptian mythology to viewers who might never have encountered it otherwise.

*Gods of Egypt*, with its depiction of the Egyptian gods and goddesses, also provides an intriguing cinematic rendition of one of Egypt's most renowned legends: the epic struggle between Horus and Set. While the film takes creative liberties in its storytelling, such as its unique portrayal of gods and the fantastical elements woven into the narrative, it still helps immortalize these ancient tales.

This reimagining of Horus's journey to reclaim his rightful throne from Set is more than just a tale of good versus evil. It encapsulates the timeless themes of power, justice, and redemption that are central to

Egyptian mythology. The film's visualization of these gods, their powers, and the mythical landscapes of ancient Egypt helps to make these ancient stories relatable to a modern audience. Even though the narrative greatly diverges from traditional mythological texts, it succeeds in capturing the essence of the dramatic and complex relationships in the Egyptian pantheon.

As for television, series like Marvel's *Moon Knight* introduce a different flavor to the portrayal of Egyptian mythology. Here, we see a blend of modern storytelling with mythological elements, bringing characters like Khonshu, the Egyptian god of the moon, into a contemporary setting. Documentaries offer a more factual and historical perspective. They usually delve into the archaeological, historical, and cultural aspects of these myths, providing a grounded and educational viewpoint.

Apart from literature and media, the influence of Egyptian mythology also made a resounding impact on the world of architecture and urban design. The Luxor Hotel, an architectural marvel in the heart of Las Vegas, is just one example that stands as a modern homage to the grandeur of ancient Egypt. Its main structure, a colossal pyramid, is an iconic feature on the Las Vegas Strip, complete with a replica of the Sphinx guarding the entrance. The hotel's design goes beyond mere replication; inside, the decor and motifs are infused with elements reminiscent of Egyptian art and mythology, from statues of gods and goddesses to giant sculptures of pharaohs. The blending of ancient symbolism with modern luxury creates an immersive experience, transporting visitors to a bygone era of pharaohs and pyramids.

In a similar vein, Sunway Pyramid in Malaysia is another striking example of Egyptian-inspired architecture. This shopping mall, distinguished by its massive lion-headed Sphinx and a pyramid, is considered a unique landmark in the city of Selangor. The mall's interior, adorned with murals, hieroglyphs, and statues, makes shopping an experience intertwined with cultural exploration.

The Louvre in Paris, renowned for its vast collection of art, features striking glass pyramids in its courtyard and houses an extensive collection of ancient Egyptian artifacts. The modern glass pyramids outside give a modern twist to the classic museum building, creating a visual dialogue between the old and the new, the ancient and the modern. Inside, visitors can experience firsthand the art, culture, and rich mythology of ancient Egypt. This space in the Louvre serves as both a tribute and a bridge, connecting contemporary viewers to the distant past of the Egyptian civilization.

In addition to architectural landmarks in various countries, Egyptian motifs have also found their way into public art and spaces, further illustrating the pervasive influence of this ancient civilization. For instance, in several metropolitan areas, one might encounter sculptures or murals depicting Egyptian deities or symbols like the Eye of Horus, an ancient Egyptian symbol of protection, royal power, and good health. There might even be representations of pharaonic iconography. These pieces of art, whether in the form of a standalone sculpture in a park or a detailed mural on a city wall, bring a touch of ancient mystique to modern public spaces. They serve as visual reminders of the enduring legacy of Egyptian culture and its capacity to inspire artists across generations and regions.

These symbols from Egyptian mythology are part of our daily lives, often without us even realizing it. The ankh, known as the key of life, is frequently seen in various forms of jewelry, fashion, and even in popular media, symbolizing life and immortality.

While direct phrases and references from Egyptian mythology are less common in everyday language compared to visual symbols, the impact of these myths is still evident in various cultural references. For instance, terms like "pharaoh" are often used metaphorically to represent power and authority, and references to mummies and pyramids are commonly found in popular culture.

Modern artists often draw inspiration from the rich iconography and symbolism of ancient Egypt, creating works that fuse the old and the new. These artistic endeavors range from paintings and sculptures to digital art, echoing the motifs, color schemes, and narrative elements of Egyptian mythology. For instance, artists like Judy Chicago and Ellen Gallagher have incorporated elements of Egyptian mythology in their works.

The influence of Egyptian mythology is equally striking in the world of fashion. Designers have long been fascinated by the opulence and mystique of ancient Egypt, which is often reflected in collections featuring bold prints, hieroglyphic patterns, and accessories reminiscent of Egyptian art. For instance, fashion shows have seen models adorned with Cleopatra-style headpieces and jewelry or garments that echo the regal draping of pharaonic clothing. These fashion statements are more than just a nod to historical aesthetics; they are also a modern reinterpretation of the mythological and cultural richness of Egypt.

In this journey through the echoes of Egyptian mythology in our modern world, we have seen how these ancient narratives continue to weave their magic into various aspects of contemporary culture. From the imaginative retellings in literature and the captivating representations in film and television to the architectural wonders inspired by ancient structures, these age-old stories maintain a vibrant presence. The symbols and expressions derived from these myths enrich our daily lives, and the artistic and fashion industries continue to draw inspiration from the rich Egyptian culture.

The enduring legacy of Egyptian mythology lies in its timeless appeal and the universal themes it explores. Of course, not all the stories of gods and pharaohs survived the test of time, but those that did resonate with such universality and depth that they continue to captivate us today.

# Conclusion

This exploration into the pantheon of Egyptian gods and goddesses has been more than an excursion into the past; it has also been a journey into the heart of human experience, revealing enduring themes and universal truths that resonate through time. It is safe to say that as we close the final pages of this journey, we find ourselves not at the end but rather at the beginning of a deeper understanding.

True, these gods and goddesses are no longer worshiped. In fact, even the grandest of their temples left to us are only in ruins, with some others probably still buried deep in the golden sands. Nevertheless, the narratives involving these deities continue to speak to us, highlighting the enduring relevance of ancient wisdom in our contemporary world.

The Egyptians saw the divine in almost everything, from the grandeur of the pyramids to the simplicity of the Nile's ebb and flow. This sense of interconnectedness—the belief that every element of the world is part of a greater whole—is a powerful reminder of our own connection to the universe and to each other. In our modern times, where the threat of environmental degradation looms large, this ancient worldview urges us to reconsider our relationship with nature and the importance of living in harmony with our environment.

The societal structures and spiritual practices of ancient Egypt also offer timeless lessons in governance, justice, and morality. The Egyptians' emphasis on Ma'at (the concept of truth, balance, and order) in their daily lives and in their governance clearly proved their advanced societal organization and their deep understanding of ethical living. In our world of complex social and political challenges, the Egyptian commitment to balance and harmony presents a model for creating more equitable and just societies. They remind us that leadership should be balanced with compassion, that justice requires fairness, and that our actions always have consequences.

The legends of the Egyptian gods and goddesses still speak to us today because of how they address fundamental human concerns: the mysteries of life and death, the quest for knowledge and power, the need for protection, and the search for meaning. The tales of deities like Ra, Osiris, Isis, Set, Horus, and even Serket or Thoth continue to offer comfort and guidance in our search for understanding in the face of life's uncertainties.

These myths also speak to the power of imagination and storytelling in shaping our understanding of the world and universe. They are not just wild stories where logic and science take a back seat. Yes, these legends are infused with exaggerations and creativity, but within their fantastical elements lie wisdom, truths, and insights. In these tales, the gods and mythical beings do more than just go on adventures. Their journeys also gave way for us to think and wonder.

These myths are indeed a testament to the resilience and adaptability of human cultures. They have transcended time and geography, finding relevance in different eras and societies. The ancient Egyptians might have lived in a world vastly different from ours, but their stories continue to inspire, educate, and resonate with people across the world today.

# Here's another book by Enthralling History that you might like

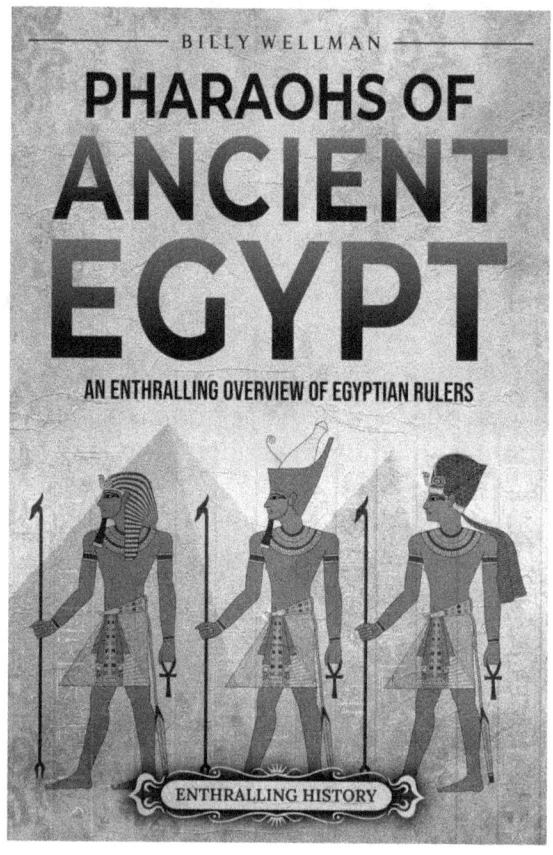

# Free limited time bonus

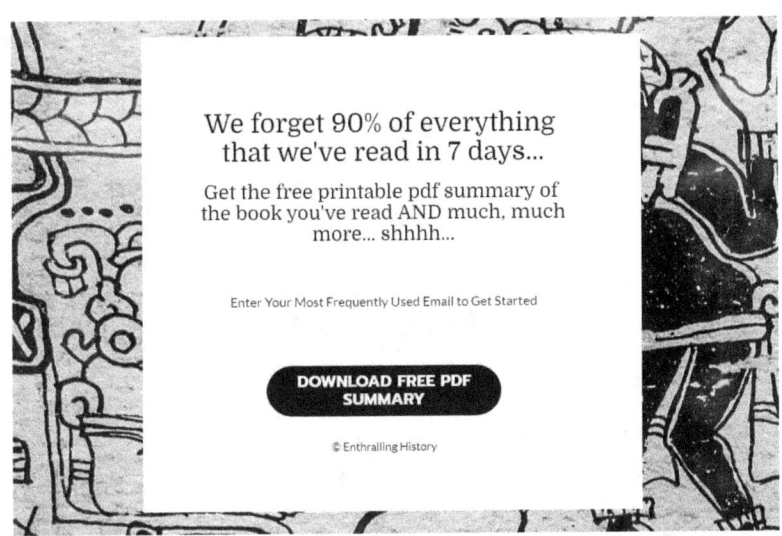

Stop for a moment. We have a free bonus set up for you. The problem is this: we forget 90% of everything that we read after 7 days. Crazy fact, right? Here's the solution: we've created a printable, 1-page pdf summary for this book that you're reading now. All you have to do to get your free pdf summary is to go to the following website:
**https://livetolearn.lpages.co/enthrallinghistory/**

Or, Scan the QR code!

Once you do, it will be intuitive. Enjoy, and thank you!

# Bibliography

*Anubis: the Jackal-Headed God of mummification and embalming.* (2022, March 21). Timeless Myths.
https://www.timelessmyths.com/gods/egyptian/anubis/

*Cult of Isis.* (n.d.).
http://persweb.wabash.edu/facstaff/royaltyr/AncientCities/web/rel%20372%20project/ISIS.htm

Debeysklenar. (2021, July 23). *The Voyage of RA.* Debeysklenar.
https://debeysklenar.wordpress.com/2016/07/31/the-voyage-of-ra/

*Egypt: Wadjet, Goddess of Lower Egypt, Papyrus, and Protector of Pharaoh.* (n.d.). http://www.touregypt.net/featurestories/wadjeta.htm

Fawn, S. (2023, March 18). *Hymn to Nut, the Sky Goddess.* Iseum Sanctuary.
https://iseumsanctuary.com/2020/09/26/hymn-to-nut-the-sky-goddess/#:~:text=O%20Nut%2C%20cast%20yourself%20upon,one%20is%20among%20your%20children

Jackson, J. (n.d.). *Egyptian Myths.* Simon and Schuster.

Jerkins, M. (2021, January 4). *Lettuce and Kings: The power struggle between Horus and Set.* Michigan Quarterly Review.
https://sites.lsa.umich.edu/mqr/2015/05/lettuce-and-kings-the-power-struggle-between-horus-and-set-2/

Joe, J. (2022, January 11). *Babi: Get to know the monkey God of ancient Egyptian mythology.* Timeless Myths.
https://www.timelessmyths.com/mythology/babi/

Klimczak, N., & Klimczak, N. (2023, March 11). *Anubis, Egyptian God of the dead and the underworld.* Ancient Origins Reconstructing the Story of

Humanity's Past. https://www.ancient-origins.net/myths-legends/anubis-jackal-god-and-guide-ancient-egyptian-afterlife-006155

Mark, J. J. (2023). Anubis. *World History Encyclopedia.* https://www.worldhistory.org/Anubis/

Mark, J. J. (2023). RA (Egyptian God). *World History Encyclopedia.* https://www.worldhistory.org/Ra_(Egyptian_God)/

Mark, J. J. (2024). Great Female Rulers of Ancient Egypt. *World History Encyclopedia.* https://www.worldhistory.org/article/1040/great-female-rulers-of-ancient-egypt/

Mark, J. J. (2024). Serket. *World History Encyclopedia.* https://www.worldhistory.org/Serket/

Mark, J. J. (2024). Seshat. *World History Encyclopedia.* https://www.worldhistory.org/Seshat/

Mark, J. J. (2024). Horus. *World History Encyclopedia.* https://www.worldhistory.org/Horus/

Maydana, S. (2023, April 6). *The Contendings of Horus and Seth: Clash of the Egyptian Titans.* TheCollector. https://www.thecollector.com/contendings-horus-and-seth-egyptian-titans/

*Nut – mythopedia.* (n.d.). Mythopedia. https://mythopedia.com/topics/nut

*Ogdoad of Hermopolis (Khmunu) | Ancient Egypt online.* (n.d.). https://ancientegyptonline.co.uk/ogdoad/

*Sobek | The Crocodile God of strength and power.* (n.d.). https://www.ancient-egypt-online.com/sobek.html

Sullivan, K., & Sullivan, K. (2023, March 11). *The mythology of Nut, Mother of Gods.* Ancient Origins Reconstructing the Story of Humanity's Past. https://www.ancient-origins.net/myths-legends/mythology-nut-mother-gods-007084

*Egyptian Mythology Creation Story.* (2021, December 1). Egypt Tours Portal. https://www.egypttoursportal.com/en-us/the-creation-of-egyptian-mythology/

*The story of RA and Isis.* (2023, July 7). The Story Museum. https://www.storymuseum.org.uk/1001-stories/the-story-of-ra-and-isis

Winters, R., & Winters, R. (2019, September 3). *The Infinite Ogdoad: the creation pantheon of ancient Egypt and predecessor gods of the Old Kingdom.* Ancient Origins Reconstructing the Story of Humanity's Past. https://www.ancient-origins.net/human-origins-religions/infinite-ogdoad-creation-pantheon-ancient-egypt-and-predecessor-gods-old-020447

# Image Sources

1  Jeff Dahl, CC BY-SA 4.0 <https://creativecommons.org/licenses/by-sa/4.0>, via Wikimedia Commons: https://commons.wikimedia.org/wiki/File:Eye_of_Ra_bw.svg

2  Dendera_Deckenrelief_02.JPG: Olaf Tauschderivative work: JMCC1 (talk)photographe/égyptologue, CC BY 3.0 <https://creativecommons.org/licenses/by/3.0>, via Wikimedia Commons: https://commons.wikimedia.org/wiki/File:L%27Ogdoade_d%27Hermopolis.jpg

3  Jeff Dahl, CC BY-SA 4.0 <https://creativecommons.org/licenses/by-sa/4.0>, via Wikimedia Commons: https://commons.wikimedia.org/wiki/File:Re-Horakhty.svg

4  Amanda Slater from Coventry, West Midlands, UK, CC BY-SA 2.0 <https://creativecommons.org/licenses/by-sa/2.0>, via Wikimedia Commons: https://commons.wikimedia.org/wiki/File:Tutankhamun_-_Treasures_of_the_Golden_Pharaoh_(49587454536).jpg

5  https://commons.wikimedia.org/wiki/File:Book_of_Gates_Barque_of_Ra_cropped.jpg

6  Eternal Space, CC BY-SA 4.0 <https://creativecommons.org/licenses/by-sa/4.0>, via Wikimedia Commons: https://commons.wikimedia.org/wiki/File:Apep_(Deity).png

7  Eternal Space, CC BY-SA 4.0 <https://creativecommons.org/licenses/by-sa/4.0>, via Wikimedia Commons: https://commons.wikimedia.org/wiki/File:Amun_(God).png

8  https://commons.wikimedia.org/wiki/File:Geb,_Nut,_Shu.jpg

9  Hans Bernhard (Schnobby), CC BY-SA 3.0 <https://creativecommons.org/licenses/by-sa/3.0>, via Wikimedia Commons: https://commons.wikimedia.org/wiki/File:Goddess_Nut_2.JPG

10 Eternal Space, CC BY-SA 4.0 <https://creativecommons.org/licenses/by-sa/4.0>, via Wikimedia Commons: https://commons.wikimedia.org/wiki/File:Set_(God).png

11 P Aculeius, CC BY-SA 3.0 <https://creativecommons.org/licenses/by-sa/3.0>, via Wikimedia Commons: https://commons.wikimedia.org/wiki/File:Sha_(animal).jpg

12 https://commons.wikimedia.org/wiki/File:Set_speared_Apep.jpg

13 derivative work: A. Parrot (talk)La_tombe_de_Horemheb_(KV.57)_(Vallée_des_Rois_Thèbes_ouest)_-4.jpg: Jean-Pierre Dalbéra, CC BY 2.0 <https://creativecommons.org/licenses/by/2.0>, via Wikimedia Commons: https://commons.wikimedia.org/wiki/File:La_Tombe_de_Horemheb_cropped.jpg

14 https://commons.wikimedia.org/wiki/File:The_judgement_of_the_dead_in_the_presence_of_Osiris.jpg

15 Louvre Museum, CC BY-SA 2.0 FR <https://creativecommons.org/licenses/by-sa/2.0/fr/deed.en>, via Wikimedia Commons: https://commons.wikimedia.org/wiki/File:Jewel_Osiris_family-E_6204-IMG_0641-gradient.jpg

16 Jeff Dahl, CC BY-SA 4.0 <https://creativecommons.org/licenses/by-sa/4.0>, via Wikimedia Commons: https://commons.wikimedia.org/wiki/File:Vulture_Crown.png

17 EternalSpace1977, CC BY-SA 4.0 <https://creativecommons.org/licenses/by-sa/4.0>, via Wikimedia Commons: https://commons.wikimedia.org/wiki/File:Isis_(goddess).png

18 Diego Delso, CC BY-SA 4.0 <https://creativecommons.org/licenses/by-sa/4.0>, via Wikimedia Commons: https://commons.wikimedia.org/wiki/File:File,_Asu%C3%A1n,_Egipto,_2022-04-01,_DD_89.jpg

19 Gary Todd from Xinzheng, China, CC0, via Wikimedia Commons: https://commons.wikimedia.org/wiki/File:Ancient_Egypt_Alabaster_Canopic_Jars_(27799088613).jpg

20 Allan Gluck, permissions ticket #2022102610001032, CC BY-SA 4.0 <https://creativecommons.org/licenses/by-sa/4.0>, via Wikimedia Commons: https://commons.wikimedia.org/wiki/File:Mummy_mask_cartonnage_Manchester_Museum_AN_6286_(2).jpg

21 https://commons.wikimedia.org/wiki/File:Anubis_attending_the_mummy_of_Sennedjem.jpg

22 https://commons.wikimedia.org/wiki/File:Egypt_dauingevekten.jpg

23 Eternal Space, CC BY-SA 4.0 <https://creativecommons.org/licenses/by-sa/4.0>, via Wikimedia Commons: https://commons.wikimedia.org/wiki/File:Maat_(Goddess).png

24 https://commons.wikimedia.org/wiki/File:Ammit_BD.jpg

25 https://commons.wikimedia.org/wiki/File:27.1_Iaru.tif

26 https://commons.wikimedia.org/wiki/File:Thoout,_Thoth_Deux_fois_Grand,_le_Second_Herm%C3%A9s,_N372.2A.jpg

27 Jeff Dahl, CC BY-SA 4.0 <https://creativecommons.org/licenses/by-sa/4.0>, via Wikimedia Commons: https://commons.wikimedia.org/wiki/File:Horus_standing.svg

28 https://commons.wikimedia.org/wiki/File:Contendings_of_Horus_and_Seth_(CBL_Pap_1.2).jpg

29 https://commons.wikimedia.org/wiki/File:Statuettes_Senusret_I_Petrie.jpg

30 Jeff Dahl, CC BY-SA 4.0 <https://creativecommons.org/licenses/by-sa/4.0>, via Wikimedia Commons: https://commons.wikimedia.org/wiki/File:Double_crown.svg

31 Bjørn Christian Tørrissen, CC BY-SA 3.0 <https://creativecommons.org/licenses/by-sa/3.0>, via Wikimedia Commons: https://commons.wikimedia.org/wiki/File:Mask_of_Tutankhamun_2003-12-07.jpg

32 RootOfAllLight, CC BY 4.0 <https://creativecommons.org/licenses/by/4.0>, via Wikimedia Commons: https://commons.wikimedia.org/wiki/File:Wadjet_(Deity).svg

33 Onceinawhile, CC BY-SA 4.0 <https://creativecommons.org/licenses/by-sa/4.0>, via Wikimedia Commons: https://commons.wikimedia.org/wiki/File:Tomb_of_Nefertari_2022_57.jpg

34 Nekhbet, CC BY-SA 4.0 <https://creativecommons.org/licenses/by-sa/4.0>, via Wikimedia Commons: https://commons.wikimedia.org/wiki/File:Nekhbet_(Goddess).svg

35 Hedwig Storch, CC BY-SA 3.0 <https://creativecommons.org/licenses/by-sa/3.0>, via Wikimedia Commons: https://commons.wikimedia.org/wiki/File:Kom_Ombo,_Sobek_0319.JPG

36 JMCC1, CC BY-SA 3.0 <https://creativecommons.org/licenses/by-sa/3.0>, via Wikimedia Commons: https://commons.wikimedia.org/wiki/File:The_Crocodile_Museum_0288_b1.jpg

37 https://commons.wikimedia.org/wiki/File:Luxor_temple_16.jpg

38 Jeff Dahl, CC BY-SA 4.0 <https://creativecommons.org/licenses/by-sa/4.0>, via Wikimedia Commons: https://commons.wikimedia.org/wiki/File:Khnum.svg

39 Roland Unger, CC BY-SA 3.0 <https://creativecommons.org/licenses/by-sa/3.0>, via Wikimedia Commons: https://commons.wikimedia.org/wiki/File:DendaraMamisiKhnum-10.jpg

40 The Tomb of Nefetari, CC BY-SA 4.0 <https://creativecommons.org/licenses/by-sa/4.0>, via Wikimedia Commons: https://commons.wikimedia.org/wiki/File:Serket_Tomb_of_Nefetari.png

41 https://commons.wikimedia.org/wiki/File:Egyptian_-_Figure_of_Isis-Serget_as_Scorpion_-_Walters_54546_-_Side_A_(cropped).jpg

42 Heshbi, CC BY-SA 4.0 <https://creativecommons.org/licenses/by-sa/4.0>, via Wikimedia Commons: https://commons.wikimedia.org/wiki/File: Babi_(Egyptian_god).png

www.ingramcontent.com/pod-product-compliance
Lightning Source LLC
Chambersburg PA
CBHW070340010526
44107CB00004B/562